THE TRAGEDY OF
JULIUS CAESAR

Globe Book Company
A Division of Simon & Schuster
Englewood Cliffs, New Jersey

AN ADAPTED CLASSIC

THE TRAGEDY OF
JULIUS CAESAR

WILLIAM SHAKESPEARE

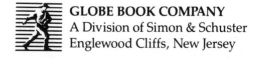
GLOBE BOOK COMPANY
A Division of Simon & Schuster
Englewood Cliffs, New Jersey

Cover designer: Marek Antoniak
Cover illustration: John Canizzo
Interior photos: Museum of Modern Art/Film Stills Archive

ISBN: 0-83590-018-5

Printed in the United States of America
1 2 3 4 5 6 7 8 9 0

Globe Book Company
A Division of Simon & Schuster
Englewood Cliffs, New Jersey

ABOUT THE AUTHOR

William Shakespeare was born in Stratford-on-Avon, England, in 1564. It is believed that he attended school there, although there are no records to prove it. Records do show that he married and had children, and that by 1592 he was working as an actor and playwright in London.

During his years in London, Shakespeare belonged to an organization that put on plays. He was one of the company's actors, although apparently not a great star as an actor. Much more important were the plays, 37 in all, that he wrote for the company. In his time, the success of these plays made him a wealthy man.

About 1612, Shakespeare retired from the theater and returned to Stratford. He died there in 1616. After his death, his friends and admirers gathered copies of all his plays and had them published in one volume, the so-called First Folio of 1623. Today these plays stand as the greatest body of writing by one man in the English language, and perhaps in any language.

ADAPTOR'S NOTE

In preparing this edition of *Julius Caesar* all of Shakespeare's original language has been kept. Extensive footnotes, summaries, and prereading material have been included in order to make Shakespeare's vocabulary and story accessible to the modern reader.

CONTENTS

INTRODUCTION

Background

Julius Caesar, a tragedy by William Shakespeare, is based on the history and politics of Rome between the years 100 and 44 B.C. Why would this 16th-century English playwright be interested in writing about the politics of ancient Rome? First, Shakespeare knew that his audiences liked a good story, with plenty of bloodshed and violence. Shakespeare also used the events in Roman history to reveal insights into human nature and the politics of any period.

Caesar was one of the greatest rulers of all time. As a Roman statesman, he began many reforms. He improved the calendar. He tried to control dishonest practices in the government. He was a powerful orator and great writer who provided the poor people of Rome with ways to improve their lives. But he did not show proper respect for the Roman Senate, and the senators resented it. Caesar compared himself to the gods. To many people, he was a tyrant whose rule threatened hundreds of years of representative government in Rome.

Caesar knew that in order to gain greater fame, he needed to win military victories. These victories made Caesar, along with Pompey, a popular general, and Crassus, a rich nobleman, the triumvirs, or three equal rulers, of Rome. In 58 B.C. Caesar entered Gaul (France) with his armies and drove out the Germans. The people of Rome rejoiced as Caesar added to the vast Roman empire. But after Crassus was defeated in battle and then murdered, Pompey, Caesar's only remaining rival for power, challenged him to surrender. Instead, Caesar attacked and began a civil war ending years later with the defeat of Pompey's army. The play opens in 45 B.C. just after Caesar has defeated Pompey's two sons in Spain.

Although Shakespeare used Caesar's name in the title of the play, readers often argue about who the real tragic hero is. Is it Caesar, who is murdered? Is it Brutus, his loyal advisor and friend, who falls into Cassius's trap of conspiracy? Or is it Mark Antony, who set out to destroy the conspirators? As you read the play, decide for yourself who the real tragic hero is.

Themes

The most important theme in *Julius Caesar* has to do with tyranny and rebellion. This theme pervades the action and is the basis for the plot of the play. The belief in fate and how the characters deal with dreams, omens, superstitions, and prophesies is another theme. In Shakespeare's time, people used superstitions — ghosts, storms, strange animals and unusual natural happenings — to guide their behavior. Look for the characters' reactions to superstitions in the play. Deceit and the use of language to manipulate is another theme to consider. Ask youself as you read, "What is the character really saying and why is he saying it?" The events in the play demonstrate how a breakdown in loyalty and friendship between people can result in world chaos. Look for examples of this theme as well as the others as you read the play.

Language

Most of *Julius Caesar* is written in blank verse. Shakespeare's blank verse is unrhymed iambic pentameter, which is usually made up of lines that are ten or eleven syllables long with a strong accent on every other syllable. Try reading the following line from *Julius Caesar* stressing the underlined syllables:

"I <u>come</u> to <u>bur</u>-y <u>Cae</u>-sar <u>not</u> to <u>praise</u> him."

How many stressed syllables did you hear?

Each new line of blank verse begins with a capital letter, unlike prose, in which the first word of each sentence begins with a capital letter and the lines are run together. Shakespeare used prose for words spoken to or by commoners, to give specific information, and for documents and letters.

DRAMATIS PERSONAE

JULIUS CAESAR
CALPURNIA, *Caesar's wife*
MARK ANTONY,
OCTAVIUS CAESAR, } *triumvirs after Caesar's death*
LEPIDUS,

MARCUS BRUTUS
PORTIA, *Brutus' wife*
CAIUS CASSIUS,
CASCA,
DECIUS BRUTUS,
CINNA, } *conspirators with Brutus*
METELLUS CIMBER,
TREBONIUS,
CAIUS LIGARIUS,

CICERO,
PUBLIUS, } *senators*
POPILIUS LENA,
FLAVIUS,
MARULLUS, } *tribunes of the people*

SOOTHSAYER
ARTEMIDORUS, *a teacher of rhetoric*
CINNA, *a poet*
Another POET

LUCILIUS,
TITINIUS,
MESSALA,
YOUNG CATO,
VOLUMNIUS,
VARRO,
CLAUDIUS,
CLITUS,
DARDANIUS,
LABEO,
FLAVIUS,
} *officers and soldiers in the army of Brutus and Cassius*

PINDARUS, *Cassius' servant*

LUCIUS,
STRATO,
} *Brutus' servants*

Caesar's SERVANT
Antony's SERVANT
Octavius' SERVANT

CARPENTER
COBBLER
Five PLEBEIANS
Three SOLDIERS *in Brutus' army*
Two SOLDIERS *in Antony's army*
MESSENGER

GHOST *of Caesar*

Senators, Plebeians, Officers, Soldiers, and Attendants

SCENE: Rome; near Sardis; near Philippi

---◆---

Before You Read Act I, Scene 1

As Scene 1 opens, Flavius and Marullus, two tribunes, attempt to break up a crowd of commoners. These people have gathered on a street to celebrate Caesar's defeat of Pompey's two sons. Flavius scolds the people for not carrying the tools of their trade as required by law "on a laboring day." When Flavius asks one man, a shoemaker, what work he does, he says that he is ". . .a mender of bad soles." This not only provides us with a pun on the words "soles" and "souls," but also foreshadows the events to come in the play. Tribunes were appointed to represent the common people. Here, the tribunes try to turn the crowd against Caesar, who has become too powerful. Note what Marullus says about the loyalty of the people.

---◆---

ACT I. Scene 1.

Location: Rome. A street.

[*Enter* FLAVIUS, MARULLUS, *and certain*
COMMONERS *over the stage*]

FLAVIUS.
Hence! Home, you idle creatures, get you home!
Is this a holiday? What, know you not,
Being mechanical, you ought not walk [1]
Upon a laboring day without the sign [2]
Of your profession? Speak, what trade art thou?

CARPENTER.
Why, sir, a carpenter.

MARULLUS.
Where is thy leather apron and thy rule?
What dost thou with thy best apparel on?
You, sir, what trade are you?

COBBLER.
Truly, sir, in respect of a fine workman, [3] I am but,
as you would say, a cobbler. [4]

MARULLUS.
But what trade art thou? Answer me directly.

---

1. **mechanical.** of the working class
2. **sign ... profession.** work clothes and tools
3. **in ... workman.** as far as skilled work is concerned
4. **cobbler.** shoemaker, or a worker who is clumsy

COBBLER.
A trade, sir, that I hope I may use with a safe conscience, which is indeed, sir, a mender of bad soles. [5]

FLAVIUS.
What trade, thou knave? Thou naughty knave, [6] what trade?

COBBLER.
Nay, I beseech you, sir, be not out with me. Yet if you be out, [7] sir, I can mend you. [8]

MARULLUS.
What mean'st thou by that? Mend me, thou saucy fellow?

COBBLER.
Why, sir, cobble you.

FLAVIUS.
Thou art a cobbler, art thou?

COBBLER.
Truly, sir, all that I live by is with the awl. [9] I meddle with no tradesman's matters nor women's matters, but withal [10] I am indeed, sir, a surgeon to old shoes. When they are in great danger, I recover [11]

---

5. **soles.** pun on "souls"
6. **naughty knave.** good-for-nothing rascal
7. **be not out ... out.** don't be angry. But if your shoes are worn out
8. **mend you.** fix your shoes (correct your faults)
9. **awl.** a tool for making holes in leather
10. **withal.** yet (pun on "with awl")
11. **recover.** resole or cure

them. As proper ^{12} men as ever trod upon neat's
leather ^{13} have gone ^{14} upon my handiwork.

FLAVIUS.
But wherefore art not in thy shop today?
Why dost thou lead these men about the streets?

COBBLER.
Truly, sir, to wear out their shoes, to get myself into
more work. But indeed, sir, we make holiday to see
Caesar and to rejoice in his triumph. ^{15}

MARULLUS.
Wherefore rejoice? What conquest brings he
 home?
What tributaries follow him to Rome ^{16}
To grace in captive bonds his chariot wheels?
You blocks, you stones, you worse than senseless
 things!
O you hard hearts, you cruel men of Rome,
Knew you not Pompey? Many a time and oft ^{17}

---

12. **proper.** handsome
13. **as ... leather.** as ever wore shoes.
    neat's leather. cowhide
14. **gone.** walked
15. **triumph.** triumphal procession to honor a victorious
    general and his army
16. **tributaries.** captives who will pay ransom for their
    release
17. **Pompey.** a Roman general and triumvir, defeated by
    Caesar in 48 B.C., who fled to Egypt where he was later
    murdered

Have you climbed up to walls and battlements,
To towers and windows, yea, to chimney tops, [18]
Your infants in your arms, and there have sat
The livelong day, with patient expectation,
To see great Pompey pass the streets of Rome. [19]
And when you saw his chariot but appear,
Have you not made an universal shout,
That Tiber trembled underneath her banks [20]
To hear the replication of your sounds [21]
Made in her concave shores?
And do you now put on your best attire?
And do you now cull out a holiday? [22]
And do you now strew flowers in his way
That comes in triumph over Pompey's blood? [23]
Begone!
Run to your houses, fall upon your knees,
Pray to the gods to intermit the plague [24]
That needs must light on this ingratitude. [25]

FLAVIUS.
Go, go, good countrymen, and for this fault

---

18. **battlements ... chimney tops.** These details describe a
    typical Elizabethan city or town, not an ancient Roman
    city.
19. **pass.** pass through
20. **Tiber.** the Tiber River that flows through Rome
21. **replication.** echo
22. **cull out.** select or give yourselves
23. **Pompey's blood.** Pompey's sons, whom Caesar had just
    defeated in battle
24. **intermit the plague.** stop the trouble or misfortune
25. **needs must.** must necessarily

Assemble all the poor men of your sort; [26]
Draw them to Tiber banks, and weep your tears
Into the channel, till the lowest stream
Do kiss the most exalted shores of all. [27]

> [*Exit all the* COMMONERS]

See whe'er their basest mettle be not moved. [28]
They vanish tongue-tied in their guiltiness.
Go you down that way towards the Capitol;
This way will I. Disrobe the images [29]
If you do find them decked with ceremonies. [30]

MARULLUS.
May we do so?
You know it is the Feast of Lupercal. [31]

FLAVIUS.
It is no matter. Let no images
Be hung with Caesar's trophies. I'll about [32]
And drive away the vulgar from the streets; [33]
So do you too, where you perceive them thick.
These growing feathers plucked from Caesar's wing
Will make him fly an ordinary pitch, [34]

---

26. sort. rank
27. kiss ... shores. touch the highest banks
28. See ... moved. See how even their inferior natures are
   stirred.
29. images. statues of Caesar
30. ceremonies. decorations set up by Caesar's followers
31. Feast of Lupercal. an ancient Roman religious festival
   celebrated on February 15
32. about. go about
33. vulgar. common people
34. pitch. height

Who else would soar above the view of men [35]
And keep us all in servile fearfulness.

[*Exit*]

---

35. else. otherwise

———————◆———————

Synopsis of Act I, Scene 1

In Scene 1, Shakespeare let us know that Caesar had enemies, mainly the tribunes and senators of Rome. These public officials feared that Caesar's power was a threat to their own positions. They questioned the loyalty of the people who, they say, cheered in a similar manner when Pompey had returned victorious from war.

———————◆———————

◆

Before You Read Act I, Scene 2

Another senator, Cassius, hates Caesar. Pay close attention, as you read, to the reasons why Cassius hates Caesar. These reasons tell you something important about Cassius's character. As the scene opens, Caesar enters with a crowd of friends and officials to watch the younger public officials, including Mark Antony, run the traditional race during the feast of Lupercal, a holiday celebrating the founding of Rome. An old soothsayer, or person who predicts the future, calls out a warning to Caesar, but Caesar dismisses him as a dreamer. What is the soothsayer's warning? Keep in mind, as you read the rest of the play, how Caesar responds to omens and superstitions. Caesar may not have been wise to ignore this omen.

A trumpet sounds. Cassius leaves the crowd with Brutus. This is the opportunity Cassius has been waiting for. He has decided to persuade Brutus, who is popular with the people, to lead the conspiracy. Cassius knows Brutus's feelings and thinks he will use them for his own purposes. Notice the ways in which Cassius draws Brutus into the conspiracy. How does Cassius portray Caesar to Brutus? Are these the real reasons Cassius dislikes Caesar?

The procession reappears. Notice what Caesar says that shows he does not trust Cassius. Brutus leaves and Cassius feels satisfied that he has won over Brutus. He will, however, use dishonest means to ensure that Brutus joins the conspiracy. What does he plan to do?

ACT I. Scene 2.

Location: A public square, later the same day.

[*Enter* CAESAR, ANTONY *for the course,* [1]
CALPURNIA, PORTIA, DECIUS, CICERO,
BRUTUS, CASSIUS, CASCA, *a* SOOTHSAYER;
after them, MARULLUS AND FLAVIUS;
CITIZENS *following*]

CAESAR.
Calpurnia!

CASCA.
     Peace, ho! Caesar speaks.

CAESAR.
         Calpurnia!

CALPURNIA.
Here, my lord.

CAESAR.
Stand you directly in Antonius' way
When he doth run his course. Antonius!

ANTONY.
Caesar, my lord?

CAESAR.
Forget not, in your speed, Antonius,
To touch Calpurnia; for our elders say

---

1. **for the course.** ready for the footrace that was part of
the Lupercal festivities

The barren, touchèd in this holy chase,
Shake off their sterile curse. [2]

ANTONY.
                              I shall remember.
When Caesar says "Do this," it is performed.

CAESAR.
Set on, and leave no ceremony out. [3]

SOOTHSAYER. [4]
Caesar!

CAESAR.
Ha? Who calls?

CASCA.
Bid every noise be still. Peace yet again!

                              [*The music stops*]

CAESAR.
Who is it in the press that calls on me? [5]
I hear a tongue shriller than all the music
Cry "Caesar!" Speak; Caesar is turned to hear.

SOOTHSAYER.
Beware the ides of March. [6]

---

2. **barren ... curse.** It was believed that if women who were
   unable to bear children (such as Calpurnia),were touched
   by a runner during this race, they would become fertile.
3. **Set on.** proceed
4. **Soothsayer.** one who predicts the future
5. **press.** crowd
6. **ides of March.** March 15 (According to the ancient
   Roman calendar, the 15th of every month was called the
   ides.)

CAESAR.

What man is that?

BRUTUS.
A soothsayer bids you beware the ides of March.

CAESAR.
Set him before me. Let me see his face.

CASSIUS.
Fellow, come from the throng. [*The* SOOTHSAYER *comes forward*] Look upon Caesar.

CAESAR.
What sayst thou to me now? Speak once again.

SOOTHSAYER.
Beware the ides of March.

CAESAR.
He is a dreamer. Let us leave him. Pass.

[*A trumpet sounds. Exit all but* BRUTUS *and* CASSIUS]

CASSIUS.
Will you go see the order of the course? [7]

BRUTUS.
Not I.

CASSIUS.
I pray you, do.

---

7. order of the course. ritual of the race

BRUTUS.
I am not gamesome. I do lack some part [8]
Of that quick spirit that is in Antony. [9]
Let me not hinder, Cassius, your desires;
I'll leave you.

CASSIUS.
Brutus, I do observe you now of late.
I have not from your eyes that gentleness
And show of love as I was wont to have. [10]
You bear too stubborn and too strange a hand [11]
Over your friend that loves you.

BRUTUS.
                              Cassius,
Be not deceived. If I have veiled my look, [12]
I turn the trouble of my countenance
Merely upon myself. Vexèd I am [13]
Of late with passions of some difference, [14]
Conceptions only proper to myself, [15]
Which give some soil, perhaps, to my behaviors. [16]
But let not therefore my good friends be grieved —
Among which number, Cassius, be you one —
Nor construe any further my neglect [17]

---

8. **gamesome.** fond of sports
9. **quick spirit.** lively disposition
10. **wont.** accustomed
11. **stubborn.** rough. **strange.** unfriendly
12. **veiled my look.** been unfriendly
13. **Merely.** entirely
14. **passions of some difference.** conflicting feelings
15. **only proper to myself.** that are of concern only to me
16. **soil.** blemish
17. **construe any further.** interpret otherwise

Than that poor Brutus, with himself at war,
Forgets the shows of love to other men.

CASSIUS.
Then, Brutus, I have much mistook your passion,
By means whereof this breast of mine hath buried
Thoughts of great value, worthy cogitations. [18]
Tell me, good Brutus, can you see your face?

BRUTUS.
No, Cassius, for the eye sees not itself
But by reflection, by some other things.

CASSIUS.
'Tis just. [19]
And it is very much lamented, Brutus,
That you have no such mirrors as will turn
Your hidden worthiness into your eye,
That you might see your shadow. I have heard [20]
Where many of the best respect in Rome, [21]
Except immortal Caesar, speaking of Brutus
And groaning underneath this age's yoke, [22]
Have wished that noble Brutus had his eyes. [23]

BRUTUS.
Into what dangers would you lead me, Cassius,

---

18. **I have much mistook ... cogitations.** I misunderstood
    your feelings because I have also kept thoughts to myself.
19. **'Tis just.** It is true
20. **turn ... shadow.** reflect your hidden, noble qualities so you
    could see yourself
21. **best respect.** most respected
22. **this age's yoke.** Caesar's tyrrany
23. **had his eyes.** could see through the eyes of Caesar's critics

That you would have me seek into myself
For that which is not in me?

CASSIUS.

Therefore, good Brutus, be prepared to hear;
And since you know you cannot see yourself
So well as by reflection, I, your glass, [24]
Will modestly discover to yourself
That of yourself which you yet know not of. [25]
And be not jealous on me, gentle Brutus. [26]
Were I a common laughter, or did use [27]
To stale with ordinary oaths my love
To every new protester; if you know [28]
That I do fawn on men and hug them hard
And after scandal them, or if you know [29]
That I profess myself in banqueting [30]
To all the rout, then hold me dangerous. [31]

[Flourish of trumpets and shout]

BRUTUS.
What means this shouting? I do fear the people
Choose Caesar for their king.

---

24. **glass.** mirror
25. **will modestly discover ... not of.** will tell Brutus's inner strengths and feelings without exaggeration
26. **jealous on.** suspicious of. **gentle.** noble
27. **common laughter.** object of ridicule
28. **To stale ... protester.** to cheapen my affection by swearing friendship to everyone
29. **scandal.** gossip about
30. **profess myself.** declare my friendship
31. **rout.** common people

CASSIUS.

Ay, do you fear it?
Then must I think you would not have it so.

BRUTUS.

I would not, Cassius, yet I love him well.
But wherefore do you hold me here so long?
What is it that you would impart to me?
If it be aught toward the general good,
Set honor in one eye and death i' th' other
And I will look on both indifferently; [32]
For let the gods so speed me as I love [33]
The name of honor more than I fear death.

CASSIUS.

I know that virtue to be in you, Brutus,
As well as I do know your outward favor. [34]
Well, honor is the subject of my story.
I cannot tell what you and other men
Think of this life; but, for my single self,
I had as lief not be as live to be [35]
In awe of such a thing as I myself. [36]
I was born free as Caesar, so were you;
We both have fed as well, and we can both
Endure the winter's cold as well as he.
For once, upon a raw and gusty day,
The troubled Tiber chafing with her shores, [37]

---

32. **indifferently.** without preference
33. **speed me.** make me prosper
34. **favor.** appearance
35. **as lief not be.** just as soon not exist
36. **such ... myself.** a fellow human being (Caesar)
37. **chafing with.** raging against

Caesar said to me, "Dar'st thou, Cassius, now
Leap in with me into this angry flood
And swim to yonder point?" Upon the word,
Accoutered as I was, I plungèd in [38]
And bade him follow; so indeed he did.
The torrent roared, and we did buffet it
With lusty sinews, throwing it aside
And stemming it with hearts of controversy. [39]
But ere we could arrive the point proposed, [40]
Caesar cried, "Help me, Cassius, or I sink!"
Ay, as Aeneas, our great ancestor, [41]
Did from the flames of Troy upon his shoulder
The old Anchises bear, so from the waves of Tiber
Did I the tirèd Caesar. And this man
Is now become a god, and Cassius is
A wretched creature and must bend his body [42]
If Caesar carelessly but nod on him.
He had a fever when he was in Spain,
And when the fit was on him I did mark [43]
How he did shake. 'Tis true, this god did shake.
His coward lips did from their color fly, [44]
And that same eye whose bend doth awe the world [45]

---

38. **Accoutered.** dressed in armor
39. **stemming ... controversy.** making headway against it
    with our intense rivalry
40. **arrive.** arrive at
41. **Aeneas.** hero of Virgil's epic poem, *Aeneid*, the legendary
    founder of Rome who carried his father out of burning
    Troy as it was falling to the Greeks
42. **bend his body.** bow
43. **mark.** notice
44. **His coward lips ... fly.** The color left his lips like
    cowardly soldiers fleeing from battle.
45. **bend.** glance

Did lose his luster. I did hear him groan. [46]
Ay, and that tongue of his that bade the Romans
Mark him and write his speeches in their books,
Alas, it cried, "Give me some drink, Titinius,"
As a sick girl. Ye gods, it doth amaze me
A man of such a feeble temper should [47]
So get the start of the majestic world [48]
And bear the palm alone. [49]

> [*Shout. Flourish of trumpets*]

BRUTUS.
Another general shout?
I do believe that these applauses are
For some new honors that are heaped on Caesar.

CASSIUS.
Why, man, he doth bestride the narrow world [50]
Like a Colossus, and we petty men [51]
Walk under his huge legs and peep about
To find ourselves dishonorable graves. [52]
Men at some time are masters of their fates.
The fault, dear Brutus, is not in our stars,
But in ourselves, that we are underlings.

---

46. his. its
47. feeble temper. weak physical condition
48. get the start of. become the leader of
49. palm. winner's prize
50. bestride. straddle
51. Colossus. This statue of Apollo was so tall that ships
could sail between its legs.
52. dishonorable graves. shameful deaths (because they
would not be free men)

"Brutus" and "Caesar." What should be in that
 "Caesar"?
Why should that name be sounded more than yours?
Write them together, yours is as fair a name;
Sound them, it doth become the mouth as well;
Weigh them, it is as heavy; conjure with 'em,
"Brutus" will start a spirit as soon as "Caesar." [53]
Now, in the names of all the gods at once,
Upon what meat doth this our Caesar feed [54]
That he is grown so great? Age, thou art shamed!
Rome, thou hast lost the breed of noble bloods!
When went there by an age since the great flood [55]
But it was famed with more than with one man? [56]
When could they say, till now, that talked of Rome,
That her wide walks encompassed but one man?
Now is it room indeed, and room enough, [57]
When there is in it but one only man.
O, you and I have heard our fathers say
There was a Brutus once that would have brooked [58]
Th' eternal devil to keep his state in Rome
As easily as a king. [59]

---

53. **start.** raise
54. **meat.** food
55. **flood.** In Greek mythology, a flood occurred that
    drowned everyone except for Deucalion and his wife
    Pyrrha, who were saved by Zeus for their virtue.
56. **But ... man.** but it had many heroes through its history
57. **Rome, room.** both are pronounced *room*
58. **Brutus.** Lucius Junius Brutus, who expelled the
    Tarquins and founded the Roman republic in 509 B. C.
    Brutus regarded the hero as his ancestor.
59. **brooked ... king.** Lucius Brutus would have found any
    king's rule as intolerable as the devil's.

BRUTUS.
That you do love me, I am nothing jealous. [60]
What you would work me to, I have some aim. [61]
How I have thought of this and of these times
I shall recount hereafter. For this present, [62]
I would not so (with love I might entreat you)
Be any further moved. What you have said [63]
I will consider; what you have to say
I will with patience hear, and find a time
Both meet to hear and answer such high things. [64]
Till then, my noble friend, chew upon this: [65]
Brutus had rather be a villager
Than to repute himself a son of Rome
Under these hard conditions as this time
Is like to lay upon us.

CASSIUS.
I am glad that my weak words
Have struck but thus much show of fire from
    Brutus.

[*Enter* CAESAR *and his train*]

BRUTUS.
The games are done and Caesar is returning.

CASSIUS.
As they pass by, pluck Casca by the sleeve,

---

60. am nothing jealous. have no doubt
61. work. persuade.   **aim.** idea
62. present. present moment
63. I would ... moved. I will not (in the name of friendship)
    be urged any more.
64. meet. fitting
65. chew upon. think about

And he will, after his sour fashion, tell you
What hath proceeded worthy note today. [66]

BRUTUS.
I will do so. But look you, Cassius,
The angry spot doth glow on Caesar's brow,
And all the rest look like a chidden train. [67]
Calpurnia's cheek is pale, and Cicero [68]
Looks with such ferret and such fiery eyes [69]
As we have seen him in the Capitol,
Being crossed in conference by some senators. [70]

CASSIUS.
Casca will tell us what the matter is.

CAESAR.
Antonius!

ANTONY.
Caesar?

CAESAR.
Let me have men about me that are fat,
Sleek-headed men, and such as sleep o' nights.
Yond Cassius has a lean and hungry look.
He thinks too much. Such men are dangerous.

ANTONY.
Fear him not, Caesar, he's not dangerous.
He is a noble Roman, and well given. [71]

---

66. **worthy note.** worthy of notice
67. **chidden train.** scolded, attendants
68. **Cicero.** a prominent senator and orator
69. **ferret.** a small animal like a weasel with reddish eyes
70. **crossed in conference.** opposed in debate
71. **well given.** favorably disposed (towards Caesar)

CAESAR.
Would he were fatter! But I fear him not.
Yet if my name were liable to fear,
I do not know the man I should avoid
So soon as that spare Cassius. He reads much,
He is a great observer, and he looks
Quite through the deeds of men. He loves no plays, [72]
As thou dost, Antony; he hears no music. [73]
Seldom he smiles, and smiles in such a sort [74]
As if he mocked himself and scorned his spirit
That could be moved to smile at anything.
Such men as he be never at heart's ease
Whiles they behold a greater than themselves,
And therefore are they very dangerous.
I rather tell thee what is to be feared
Than what I fear, for always I am Caesar.
Come on my right hand, for this ear is deaf,
And tell me truly what thou think'st of him.

[*A trumpet sounds. Exit* CAESAR *and his train.*
CASCA *remains with* BRUTUS *and* CASSIUS]

CASCA.
You pulled me by the cloak. [75] Would you speak with
me?

---

72. **looks ... men.** can see beyond people's actions to their
    real motives
73. **hears no music.** a sign of a sullen and dangerous
    character
74. **sort.** manner
75. **cloak.** A cloak would have been worn in Elizabethan
    England, not in ancient Rome. (Shakespeare's actors
    usually wore Elizabethan clothes, even in plays set in
    other periods in history.)

BRUTUS.
Ay, Casca. Tell us what hath chanced today, [76]
That Caesar looks so sad. [77]

CASCA.
Why, you were with him, were you not?

BRUTUS.
I should not then ask Casca what had chanced.

CASCA.
Why, there was a crown offered him; and, being
offered him, he put it by [78] with the back of his
hand, thus, and then the people fell a-shouting.

BRUTUS.
What was the second noise for?

CASCA.
Why, for that too.

CASSIUS.
They shouted thrice. What was the last cry for?

CASCA.
Why, for that too.

BRUTUS.
Was the crown offered him thrice?

---

76. chanced. happened
77. sad. serious
78. put it by. pushed it aside

CASCA.

Ay, marry, was 't, [79] and he put it by thrice, every time gentler than other, and at every putting-by mine honest [80] neighbors shouted.

CASSIUS.

Who offered him the crown?

CASCA.

Why, Antony.

BRUTUS.

Tell us the manner of it, gentle Casca. [81]

CASCA.

I can as well be hanged as tell the manner of it. It was mere foolery; I did not mark it. I saw Mark Antony offer him a crown — yet 'twas not a crown neither, 'twas one of these coronets [82] — and, as I told you, he put it by once. But for all that, to my thinking, he would fain [83] have had it. Then he offered it to him again; then he put it by again; but to my thinking he was very loath to lay his fingers off it. And then he offered it the third time. He put it the third time by, and still as [84] he refused it the rabblement hooted and clapped their chapped hands, and threw up their sweaty nightcaps, [85] and

---

79. **Ay, marry, was't.** Indeed it was
80. **honest.** worthy (spoken with contempt)
81. **gentle.** noble
82. **coronets.** ornamental bands used as smaller crowns
83. **fain.** gladly
84. **still as.** whenever
85. **nightcaps.** workers' caps

uttered such a deal of stinking breath because
Caesar refused the crown that it had almost choked
Caesar, for he swooned and fell down at it. And for
mine own part I durst not laugh for fear of opening
my lips and receiving the bad air.

CASSIUS.
But soft, I pray you. What, did Caesar swoon? [86]

CASCA.
He fell down in the marketplace, and foamed at
mouth, and was speechless.

BRUTUS.
'Tis very like. He hath the falling sickness. [87]

CASSIUS.
No, Caesar hath it not, but you and I,
And honest Casca, we have the falling sickness.

CASCA.
I know not what you mean by that, but I am sure
Caesar fell down. If the tag-rag [88] people did not
clap him and hiss him, according as he pleased and
displeased them, as they use [89] to do the players in
the theater, I am no true [90] man.

---

86. **soft.** wait a minute. **swoon.** faint
87. **like.** likely. **falling sickness.** epilepsy. (Cassius
    means that the people have become helpless under
    Caesar's rule.)
88. **tag-rag.** disreputable
89. **use.** are accustomed
90. **true.** honest

BRUTUS.
What said he when he came unto himself?

CASCA.
Marry, before he fell down, when he perceived the
common herd was glad he refused the crown, he
plucked me ope [91] his doublet [92] and offered them
his throat to cut. An I had been a man of any
occupation, [93] if I would not have taken him at a
word, I would I might go to hell among the rogues.
And so he fell. When he came to himself again, he
said if he had done or said anything amiss, he
desired their worships to think it was his infirmity.
Three or four wenches [94] where I stood cried, "Alas,
good soul!" and forgave him with all their hearts.
But there's no heed to be taken of them; if Caesar
had stabbed their mothers they would have done no
less.

BRUTUS.
And after that, he came thus sad away? [95]

CASCA.
Ay.

CASSIUS.
Did Cicero say anything?

---

91. plucked me ope. pulled open
92. doublet. Elizabethan jacket.
93. An ... occupation. if I had been a workingman (a man
   of action)
94. wenches. young women
95. sad. seriously

CASCA.
Ay, he spoke Greek.

CASSIUS.
To what effect?

CASCA.
Nay, an I tell you that, I'll ne'er look you i' the face again. But those that understood him smiled at one another and shook their heads, but, for mine own part, it was Greek to me. I could tell you more news too. Marullus and Flavius, for pulling scarves [96] off Caesar's images, are put to silence. [97] Fare you well. There was more foolery yet, if I could remember it.

CASSIUS.
Will you sup with me tonight, Casca?

CASCA.
No, I am promised forth. [98]

CASSIUS.
Will you dine with me tomorrow?

CASCA.
Ay, if I be alive, and your mind hold, and your dinner worth the eating.

---

96. scarves. decorations
97. put to silence. dismissed from office (for taking the decorations off Caesar's statues)
98. am promised forth. have a previous engagement

CASSIUS.
Good. I will expect you.

CASCA.
Do so. Farewell both.

[Exit]

BRUTUS.
What a blunt fellow is this grown to be! [99]
He was quick mettle when he went to school. [100]

CASSIUS.
So is he now in execution
Of any bold or noble enterprise,
However he put on this tardy form. [101]
This rudeness is a sauce to his good wit, [102]
Which gives men stomach to digest his words [103]
With better appetite.

BRUTUS.
And so it is. For this time I will leave you.
Tomorrow, if you please to speak with me,
I will come home to you; or, if you will,
Come home to me, and I will wait for you.

CASSIUS.
I will do so. Till then, think of the world. [104]

[Exit Brutus]

---

99. **blunt.** dull
100. **quick mettle.** lively, clever
101. **However.** however much. **tardy form.** appearance of sluggishness
102. **rudeness.** rough manner. **wit.** intellect
103. **stomach.** appetite, inclination
104. **the world.** the state of the world

Well, Brutus, thou art noble. Yet I see
Thy honorable mettle may be wrought
From that it is disposed. Therefore it is meet [105]
That noble minds keep ever with their likes;
For who so firm that cannot be seduced?
Caesar doth bear me hard, but he loves Brutus. [106]
If I were Brutus now, and he were Cassius,
He should not humor me. I will this night [107]
In several hands in at his windows throw, [108]
As if they came from several citizens,
Writings, all tending to the great opinion [109]
That Rome holds of his name, wherein obscurely
Caesar's ambition shall be glancèd at. [110]
And after this let Caesar seat him sure, [111]
For we will shake him, or worse days endure.

                                                    [*Exit*]

---

105.   **Thy honorable ... disposed.** Your ordinary nature
       can be manipulated.
106.   **bear me hard.** has a grudge against me
107.   **He.** Brutus. **humor.** win me over
108.   **several hands.** different handwritings
109.   **tending to.** pointing out
110.   **glancèd.** hinted
111.   **seat him sure.** watch out

---◆---

Synopsis of Act I, Scene 2

Cassius successfully persuaded Brutus to lead the conspiracy by pointing out Caesar's weaknesses. Brutus agreed that Caesar had been acting like a god and was treating the senators as though they were not important. Cassius said that Caesar was no better than ordinary men and was not worthy to rule. Caesar became suspicious of Cassius. Cassius decided to ensure that Brutus joined the conspiracy by writing several letters with different handwriting, hinting at Caesar's ambition, and throwing them into Brutus's window.

The feelings and motives of the characters are now obvious. Shakespeare portrays Caesar, not as a great leader, but as a vain and petty weakling. Caesar is so over-confident that he dismisses the warnings of the soothsayer. Cassius is a jealous and ambitious schemer who wants to take advantage of Brutus's reputation as an honorable man. Casca has been introduced as an important character, as is the young and athletic Antony.

---◆---

---◆---

Before You Read Act I, Scene 3

It is the evening before the ides of March. Two conspirators, Casca and Cicero, meet on a Roman street during a thunderstorm. Casca describes strange images that he sees in the storm, saying they are bad omens. Think of what effect Shakespeare intended the storm to have in this scene as Casca describes his fears, first to Cicero, and then to Cassius. Notice how Cassius turns Casca's fears to his own advantage. What is the reason behind Cassius's words? Notice the words that Cassius uses to make Caesar seem all-powerful and the rest of the people seem like inferior beings. Cinna, a tribune, who is also a conspirator, enters. He is to deliver Cassius's forged letters to Brutus's house. Is Cinna glad that Brutus will lead the conspiracy? Why?

---◆---

ACT I. Scene 3.

Location: A street.

[*Thunder and lightning. Enter, meeting,* CASCA *with his sword drawn and* CICERO]

CICERO.

Good even, Casca. Brought you Caesar home? [1]
Why are you breathless? And why stare you so?

CASCA.

Are not you moved, when all the sway of earth [2]
Shakes like a thing unfirm? O Cicero,
I have seen tempests when the scolding winds
Have rived the knotty oaks, and I have seen [3]
Th' ambitious ocean swell and rage and foam
To be exalted with the threatening clouds; [4]
But never till tonight, never till now,
Did I go through a tempest dropping fire.
Either there is a civil strife in heaven,
Or else the world, too saucy with the gods, [5]
Incenses them to send destruction.

CICERO.

Why, saw you anything more wonderful? [6]

CASCA.

A common slave — you know him well by sight —

---

1. **Brought you.** did you escort
2. **sway of earth.** natural order
3. **rived.** split
4. **exalted with.** lifted up to the level of
5. **saucy.** cold
6. **more.** else. **wonderful.** wondrous

Held up his left hand, which did flame and burn
Like twenty torches joined, and yet his hand,
Not sensible of fire, remained unscorched. [7]
Besides — I ha' not since put up my sword — [8]
Against the Capitol I met a lion, [9]
Who glazed upon me and went surly by [10]
Without annoying me. And there were drawn [11]
Upon a heap a hundred ghastly women, [12]
Transformèd with their fear, who swore they saw
Men all in fire walk up and down the streets.
And yesterday the bird of night did sit [13]
Even at noonday upon the marketplace,
Hooting and shrieking. When these prodigies [14]
Do so conjointly meet, let not men say, [15]
"These are their reasons, they are natural,"
For I believe they are portentous things
Unto the climate that they point upon. [16]

CICERO.
Indeed, it is a strange-disposèd time.
But men may construe things after their fashion, [17]

---

7. **Not sensible of.** not feeling
8. **put up.** sheathed, encased
9. **Against.** opposite or near
10. **glazed.** stared
11. **annoying.** harming **drawn ... heap.** huddled together
12. **ghastly.** pale
13. **bird of night.** owl
14. **prodigies.** strange events
15. **conjointly meet.** happen at the same time
16. **portentious ... point upon.** bad omens for the country
    in which they occur
17. **construe ... after their fashion.** interpret things in
    their own way

Clean from the purpose of the things themselves. [18]
Comes Caesar to the Capitol tomorrow?

CASCA.
He doth; for he did bid Antonius
Send word to you he would be there tomorrow.

CICERO.
Good night then, Casca. This disturbèd sky
Is not to walk in.

CASCA.
Farewell, Cicero.

[*Exit* CICERO]

[*Enter* CASSIUS]

CASSIUS.
Who's there?

CASCA.
A Roman.

CASSIUS.
Casca, by your voice.

CASCA.
Your ear is good. Cassius, what night is this! [19]

CASSIUS.
A very pleasing night to honest men.

---

18. **Clean ... purpose.** different from the actual meaning
19. **what night.** what a night

CASCA.
Who ever knew the heavens menace so?

CASSIUS.
Those that have known the earth so full of faults.
For my part, I have walked about the streets,
Submitting me unto the perilous night,
And thus unbracèd, Casca, as you see, [20]
Have bared my bosom to the thunder-stone; [21]
And when the cross blue lightning seemed to open [22]
The breast of heaven, I did present myself
Even in the aim and very flash of it. [23]

CASCA.
But wherefore did you so much tempt the heavens?
It is the part of men to fear and tremble [24]
When the most mighty gods by tokens send [25]
Such dreadful heralds to astonish us. [26]

CASSIUS.
You are dull, Casca, and those sparks of life
That should be in a Roman you do want, [27]
Or else you use not. You look pale, and gaze,
And put on fear, and cast yourself in wonder, [28]

---

20. **unbracèd.** with jacket opened
21. **thunder-stone.** thunderbolt
22. **cross.** zigzag
23. **Even in the aim.** at the exact place at which it was aimed
24. **part.** role
25. **tokens.** signs
26. **astonish.** stun
27. **want.** lack
28. **put on ... in wonder.** show fear and are amazed

To see the strange impatience of the heavens.
But if you would consider the true cause
Why all these fires, why all these gliding ghosts,
Why birds and beasts from quality and kind, [29]
Why old men, fools, and children calculate, [30]
Why all these things change from their ordinance, [31]
Their natures, and preformèd faculties, [32]
To monstrous quality — why, you shall find [33]
That heaven hath infused them with these spirits
To make them instruments of fear and warning
Unto some monstrous state. [34]
Now could I, Casca, name to thee a man
Most like this dreadful night,
That thunders, lightens, opens graves, and roars
As doth the lion in the Capitol —
A man no mightier than thyself or me
In personal action, yet prodigious grown [35]
And fearful, as these strange eruptions are. [36]

CASCA.
'Tis Caesar that you mean, is it not, Cassius?

CASSIUS.
Let it be who it is. For Romans now

---

29. from ... kind. acting contrary to their nature
30. calculate. make predictions
31. ordinance. regular behavior
32. preformèd faculties. instinctual behavior
33. monstrous. unnatural
34. monstrous state. unnatural condition of government
35. prodigious grown. become huge and ominous
36. fearful. causing fear

Have thews and limbs like to their ancestors; [37]
But, woe the while, our fathers' minds are dead, [38]
And we are governed with our mothers' spirits.
Our yoke and sufferance show us womanish. [39]

CASCA.

Indeed, they say the senators tomorrow
Mean to establish Caesar as a king,
And he shall wear his crown by sea and land
In every place save here in Italy.

CASSIUS.

I know where I will wear this dagger then;
Cassius from bondage will deliver Cassius. [40]
Therein, ye gods, you make the weak most strong;
Therein, ye gods, you tyrants do defeat.
Nor stony tower, nor walls of beaten brass, [41]
Nor airless dungeon, nor strong links of iron,
Can be retentive to the strength of spirit; [42]
But life, being weary of these worldly bars, [43]
Never lacks power to dismiss itself.
If I know this, know all the world besides, [44]
that part of tyranny that I do bear
I can shake off at pleasure.

---

37. thews. muscles. **like.** similar
38. woe the while. alas for the times
39. yoke and sufferance. slavery and meek acceptance of it
40. Cassius ... will deliver Cassius. Cassius will kill
   himself rather than submit to Caesar.
41. Nor. neither
42. be ... spirit. confine a determined spirit
43. bars. prison bars (burdens, such as tyranny)
44. know ... besides. let the rest of the world know

[*Thunder still*]

CASCA.

So can I.
So every bondman in his own hand bears
The power to cancel his captivity.

CASSIUS.

And why should Caesar be a tyrant, then?
Poor man, I know he would not be a wolf
But that he sees the Romans are but sheep;
He were no lion, were not Romans hinds. [45]
Those that with haste will make a mighty fire
Begin it with weak straws. What trash is Rome,
What rubbish and what offal, when it serves [46]
For the base matter to illuminate [47]
So vile a thing as Caesar! But, O grief,
Where hast thou led me? I perhaps speak this
Before a willing bondman; then I know [48]
My answer must be made. But I am armed,
And dangers are to me indifferent. [49]

CASCA.

You speak to Casca, and to such a man
That is no fleering telltale. Hold. My hand. [50]

---

45. hinds. female deer (peasants, servants)
46. offal. garbage
47. base matter. fuel
48. a willing bondman. (Cassius suggests that Casca,
     unlike himself, accepts slavery under Caesar and might
     therefore inform on him.)
49. indifferent. unimportant
50. fleering telltale. sneering tattletale. **Hold. My hand.**
     enough; here is my hand

Be factious for redress of all these griefs, [51]
And I will set this foot of mine as far
As who goes farthest.

> [*They shake hands*]

CASSIUS.
>   There's a bargain made.
Now know you, Casca, I have moved already [52]
Some certain of the noblest-minded Romans
To undergo with me an enterprise
Of honorable-dangerous consequence;
And I do know by this they stay for me [53]
In Pompey's porch. For now, this fearful night, [54]
There is no stir or walking in the streets,
And the complexion of the element [55]
In favor's like the work we have in hand, [56]
Most bloody, fiery, and most terrible.

[*Enter* CINNA]

CASCA.
Stand close awhile, for here comes one in haste. [57]

CASSIUS.
'Tis Cinna; I do know him by his gait.
He is a friend. — Cinna, where haste you so?

---

51. **be factious.** form a faction, or group. **griefs.** grievances
52. **moved.** urged
53. **by this.** by this time. **stay.** wait
54. **Pompey's porch.** entrance to the great open theater that was built by Pompey
55. **complexion of the element.** condition of the sky
56. **In favor's like.** in appearance is like
57. **close.** hidden

CINNA.

To find out you. Who's that? Metellus Cimber?

CASSIUS.

No, it is Casca, one incorporate [58]
To our attempts. Am I not stayed for, Cinna?

CINNA.

I am glad on 't. What a fearful night is this! [59]
There's two or three of us have seen strange sights.

CASSIUS.

Am I not stayed for? Tell me.

CINNA.

Yes, you are.
O Cassius, if you could
But win the noble Brutus to our party —

CASSIUS.

Be you content. Good Cinna, take this paper,
And look you lay it in the praetor's chair, [60]
Where Brutus may but find it. And throw this [61]
In at his window. Set this up with wax
Upon old Brutus' statue. All this done, [62]
Repair to Pompey's porch, where you shall find us. [63]
Is Decius Brutus and Trebonius there?

---

58. incorporate To. united with us in
59. on 't. of it
60. praetor's chair. Roman magistrate's chair. (Brutus was a praetor.)
61. Where ... it. where only Brutus will find it
62. old Brutus. Lucius Junius Brutus, the founder of the republic of Rome
63. Repair. proceed

CINNA.
All but Metellus Cimber, and he's gone
To seek you at your house. Well, I will hie, [64]
And so bestow these papers as you bade me.

CASSIUS.
That done, repair to Pompey's theater.

[*Exit* CINNA]

Come, Casca, you and I will yet ere day
See Brutus at his house. Three parts of him [65]
Is ours already, and the man entire
Upon the next encounter yields him ours.

CASCA.
O, he sits high in all the people's hearts;
And that which would appear offense in us,
His countenance, like richest alchemy, [66]
Will change to virtue and to worthiness.

CASSIUS.
Him and his worth, and our great need of him,
You have right well conceited. Let us go, [67]
For it is after midnight, and ere day
We will awake him and be sure of him.

[*Exit*]

---

64. **hie.** go quickly
65. **parts.** quarters
66. **countenance.** support.   **alchemy.** an early form of
   chemistry in which the goal was to change baser metals
   into gold
67. **conceited.** understood

————————◆————————

Synopsis of Act I, Scene 3

Casca met with Cicero during a storm. Casca thought the storm was a bad omen and Cicero agreed that strange things were happening. He asked if Caesar would be at the Capitol the next day. Cassius entered and spoke to Casca about the meaning of the storm. Cinna joined them and Cassius asked him to deliver a letter to Brutus. They agreed to meet early the next day at Brutus's house.

————————◆————————

---◆---

Before You Read Act II, Scene 1

This act opens in Brutus's house a few hours before daybreak on the ides of March. Brutus cannot sleep. He is thinking over his conversation with Cassius during their previous meeting. Brutus wonders about his reasons for agreeing to Caesar's murder. Even though he has no personal reasons for killing Caesar, he agrees it must be done. Notice why he finally decides to join the conspiracy. Think about whether the forged letter had the effect that Cassius intended.

Cassius and the other conspirators then arrive at Brutus's house. As they begin to plan the events to take place later that day at the Capitol, Brutus clearly takes the lead. Note the three important decisions Brutus makes. Ask yourself whether it is wise that the conspirators do not take an oath of loyalty. Pay attention to the reasons given for not allowing Cicero to be included in the plot. Notice why Brutus says that Mark Antony should not be killed along with Caesar.

Final plans are set as Portia, Brutus's wife, enters the room. She complains that Brutus has not told her what is troubling him. Why does she feel she should be told what is in his heart and on his mind? What does Portia do to prove to Brutus that she can be trusted? Does Brutus agree to reveal his secrets to her?

◆

ACT II. Scene 1.

Location: Rome. Brutus' orchard, or garden.

[*Enter* BRUTUS *in his orchard*]

BRUTUS.
What, Lucius, ho! —
I cannot by the progress of the stars
Give guess how near to day. — Lucius, I say!
I would it were my fault to sleep so soundly.
When, Lucius, when? Awake, I say! What, Lucius!

[*Enter* LUCIUS]

LUCIUS.
Called you, my lord?

BRUTUS.
Get me a taper in my study, Lucius. [1]
When it is lighted, come and call me here.

LUCIUS.
I will, my lord.

[*Exit*]

BRUTUS.
It must be by his death. And for my part
I know no personal cause to spurn at him, [2]
But for the general. He would be crowned. [3]
How that might change his nature, there's the
  question.

---

1. **Get me.** put.   **taper.** candle
2. **spurn.** kick
3. **general.** public good

It is the bright day that brings forth the adder,
And that craves wary walking. Crown him that, [4]
And then I grant we put a sting in him
That at his will he may do danger with.
Th' abuse of greatness is when it disjoins
Remorse from power. And to speak truth of Caesar, [5]
I have not known when his affections swayed [6]
More than his reason. But 'tis a common proof [7]
That lowliness is young ambition's ladder, [8]
Whereto the climber-upward turns his face;
But when he once attains the upmost round [9]
He then unto the ladder turns his back,
Looks in the clouds, scorning the base degrees [10]
By which he did ascend. So Caesar may.
Then, lest he may, prevent. And since the quarrel
Will bear no color for the thing he is, [11]
Fashion it thus: that what he is, augmented, [12]
Would run to these and these extremities. [13]
And therefore think him as a serpent's egg
Which, hatched, would, as his kind, grow
    mischievous;
And kill him in the shell.

---

4. **craves.** requires.   **that.** king, emperor
5. **Remorse.** compassion
6. **affections swayed.** passions ruled
7. **proof.** experience
8. **lowliness.** pretended humility
9. **round.** rung (the crown)
10. **base degrees.** lower rungs or people in lower positions
11. **the quarrel ... no color.** Our complaint cannot be
    justified in view of what he is now.
12. **Fashion it.** state the case
13. **extremities.** extremes (of tyranny)

[*Enter* LUCIUS]

LUCIUS.
The taper burneth in your closet, sir. [14]
Searching the window for a flint, I found
This paper, thus sealed up, and I am sure
It did not lie there when I went to bed.

[*Gives him the letter*]

BRUTUS.
Get you to bed again. It is not day.
Is not tomorrow, boy, the ides of March? [15]

LUCIUS.
I know not, sir.

BRUTUS.
Look in the calendar and bring me word.

LUCIUS.
I will, sir.

[*Exit*]

BRUTUS.
The exhalations whizzing in the air [16]
Give so much light that I may read by them.
[*Opens the letter and reads*]
"Brutus, thou sleep'st. Awake, and see thyself!
Shall Rome, et cetera . . . Speak, strike, redress!"
"Brutus, thou sleep'st. Awake!"
Such instigations have been often dropped
Where I have took them up.

---

14. **closet.** study
15. **ides.** fifteenth day
16. **exhalations.** meteors

"Shall Rome, et cetera . . ." Thus must I piece it out:
Shall Rome stand under one man's awe? What,
    Rome?
My ancestors did from the streets of Rome
The Tarquin drive, when he was called a king.
"Speak, strike, redress!" Am I entreated
To speak and strike? O Rome, I make thee
    promise, [17]
If the redress will follow, thou receivest [18]
Thy full petition at the hand of Brutus.

[*Enter* LUCIUS]

LUCIUS.
Sir, March is wasted fifteen days. [*Knock within*]

BRUTUS.
'Tis good. Go to the gate; somebody knocks.

                    [*Exit* LUCIUS]

Since Cassius first did whet me against Caesar, [19]
I have not slept.
Between the acting of a dreadful thing
And the first motion, all the interim is [20]
Like a phantasma or a hideous dream. [21]
The genius and the mortal instruments [22]

---

17. **I make thee promise.** I promise thee
18. **If ... follow.** if striking down Caesar will lead to changes
19. **whet.** incite
20. **motion.** proposal
21. **phantasma.** nightmare
22. **The genius ... council.** man's rational nature is in
    conflict with the part that takes action

Are then in council; and the state of man,
Like to a little kingdom, suffers then
The nature of an insurrection. [23]

[*Enter* LUCIUS]

LUCIUS.
Sir, 'tis your brother Cassius at the door, [24]
Who doth desire to see you.

BRUTUS.

Is he alone?

LUCIUS.
No, sir, there are more with him.

BRUTUS.

Do you know them?

LUCIUS.
No, sir. Their hats are plucked about their ears,
And half their faces buried in their cloaks,
That by no means I may discover them [25]
By any mark of favor. [26]

BRUTUS.

Let 'em enter.
[*Exit* LUCIUS]
They are the faction. O conspiracy,
Sham'st thou to show thy dangerous brow by night,

---

23. insurrection. revolt
24. brother. brother-in-law. (Cassius had married one of
   Brutus's sisters.)
25. discover. identify
26. By ... favor. by their appearance

When evils are most free? O, then by day [27]
Where wilt thou find a cavern dark enough
To mask thy monstrous visage? Seek none,
   conspiracy!
Hide it in smiles and affability;
For if thou path, thy native semblance on, [28]
Not Erebus itself were dim enough [29]
To hide thee from prevention. [30]

[*Enter the conspirators,* CASSIUS, CASCA,
DECIUS, CINNA, METELLUS CIMBER, *and*
TREBONIUS]

CASSIUS.

I think we are too bold upon your rest. [31]
Good morrow, Brutus. Do we trouble you?

BRUTUS.

I have been up this hour, awake all night.
Know I these men that come along with you?

CASSIUS.

Yes, every man of them, and no man here
But honors you; and every one doth wish
You had but that opinion of yourself
Which every noble Roman bears of you.
This is Trebonius.

---

27. **free.** free to roam at will
28. **path.** proceed, walk about.   **thy ... on.** looking as you
   normally do
29. **Erebus.** The dark place between earth and Hades
30. **prevention.** being discovered and stopped
31. **upon.** in interfering with

BRUTUS.

                   He is welcome hither.

CASSIUS.

  This, Decius Brutus.

BRUTUS.

                   He is welcome too.

CASSIUS.

  This, Casca; this, Cinna; and this, Metellus
    Cimber.

BRUTUS.

  They are all welcome.
  What watchful cares do interpose themselves
  Betwixt your eyes and night? [32]

CASSIUS.

  Shall I entreat a word?

             [BRUTUS *and* CASSIUS *whisper*]

DECIUS.

  Here lies the east. Doth not the day break here?

CASCA.

  No.

CINNA.

  O, pardon, sir, it doth; and yon gray lines
  That fret the clouds are messengers of day. [33]

---

32. What watchful ... night. What worries keep you awake?
33. fret. decorate

CASCA.

You shall confess that you are both deceived. [34]
Here, as I point my sword, the sun arises,
Which is a great way growing on the south, [35]
Weighing the youthful season of the year. [36]
Some two months hence, up higher toward the
    north
He first presents his fire; and the high east [37]
Stands, as the Capitol, directly here.

BRUTUS.

[*Coming forward*]

Give me your hands all over, one by one. [38]

CASSIUS.

And let us swear our resolution.

BRUTUS.

No, not an oath. If not the face of men, [39]
The sufferance of our souls, the time's abuse — [40]
If these be motives weak, break off betimes, [41]
And every man hence to his idle bed; [42]
So let high-sighted tyranny range on [43]

---

34. deceived. mistaken
35. growing on. tending toward
36. Weighing. considering
37. the high. due
38. all over. one and all
39. face of men. the sadness on men's faces
40. sufferance. suffering. **time's abuse.** corruptions of
    the present day
41. betimes. quickly
42. idle. unused, empty
43. high-sighted. arrogant

Till each man drop by lottery. But if these, [44]
(As I am sure they do) bear fire enough
To kindle cowards and to steel with valor
The melting spirits of women, then, countrymen,
What need we any spur but our own cause
To prick us to redress? What other bond [45]
Than secret Romans that have spoke the word
And will not palter? And what other oath [46]
Than honesty to honesty engaged [47]
That this shall be or we will fall for it?
Swear priests and cowards and men cautelous, [48]
Old feeble carrions, and such suffering souls [49]
That welcome wrongs; unto bad causes swear
Such creatures as men doubt; but do not stain
The even virtue of our enterprise, [50]
Nor th' insuppressive mettle of our spirits, [51]
To think that or our cause or our performance [52]
Did need an oath, when every drop of blood
That every Roman bears — and nobly bears —
Is guilty of a several bastardy [53]
If he do break the smallest particle
Of any promise that hath passed from him.

---

44. **by lottery.** by chance. **these.** these injustices just
    mentioned
45. **prick us to redress.** spur us on to correct these evils
46. **palter.** talk insincerely
47. **honesty engaged.** personal honor pledged
48. **Swear.** make swear **cautelous.** cautious
49. **carrions.** men who look like decaying corpses
50. **even.** constant
51. **insuppressive mettle.** uncrushable courage
52. **or ... or.** either our cause or
53. **Is guilty ... bastardy.** is no true Roman

CASSIUS.

But what of Cicero? Shall we sound him? [54]
I think he will stand very strong with us.

CASCA.

Let us not leave him out.

CINNA.

No, by no means.

METELLUS.

O, let us have him, for his silver hairs
Will purchase us a good opinion [55]
And buy men's voices to commend our deeds.
It shall be said his judgment ruled our hands;
Our youths and wildness shall no whit appear, [56]
But all be buried in his gravity.

BRUTUS.

O, name him not. Let us not break with him, [57]
For he will never follow anything
That other men begin.

CASSIUS.

Then leave him out.

CASCA.

Indeed he is not fit.

DECIUS.

Shall no man else be touched but only Caesar?

---

54. **sound him.** find out his opinions
55. **purchase.** bring
56. **no whit.** not the least bit
57. **break with.** confide in

CASSIUS.

Decius, well urged. I think it is not meet [58]
Mark Antony, so well beloved of Caesar,
Should outlive Caesar. We shall find of him [59]
A shrewd contriver; and you know his means,
If he improve them, may well stretch so far [60]
As to annoy us all. Which to prevent, [61]
Let Antony and Caesar fall together.

BRUTUS.

Our course will seem too bloody, Caius Cassius,
To cut the head off and then hack the limbs,
Like wrath in death and envy afterwards; [62]
For Antony is but a limb of Caesar.
Let's be sacrificers, but not butchers, Caius.
We all stand up against the spirit of Caesar,
And in the spirit of men there is no blood.
O, that we then could come by Caesar's spirit [63]
And not dismember Caesar! But, alas,
Caesar must bleed for it. And, gentle friends, [64]
Let's kill him boldly but not wrathfully;
Let's carve him as a dish fit for the gods,
Not hew him as a carcass fit for hounds.
And let our hearts, as subtle masters do,

---

58. meet. fitting
59. of. in
60. improve. increase
61. annoy. hurt
62. Like ... afterwards. as if killing in anger and feeling
hatred afterwards
63. come by Caesar's spirit. get hold of the principles of
tyranny for which Caesar stands
64. gentle. honorable

Stir up their servants to an act of rage [65]
And after seem to chide 'em. This shall make [66]
Our purpose necessary, and not envious; [67]
Which so appearing to the common eyes,
We shall be called purgers, not murderers.
And for Mark Antony, think not of him;
For he can do no more than Caesar's arm
When Caesar's head is off.

CASSIUS.

                    Yet I fear him,
For in the engrafted love he bears to Caesar — [68]

BRUTUS.

Alas, good Cassius, do not think of him.
If he love Caesar, all that he can do
Is to himself — take thought and die for Caesar. [69]
And that were much he should, for he is given [70]
To sports, to wildness, and much company.

TREBONIUS.

There is no fear in him. Let him not die, [71]
For he will live, and laugh at this hereafter.
                                [Clock strikes]

---

65. their servants. our hands
66. chide 'em. scold them
67. envious. malicious
68. engrafted. firmly rooted
69. take thought. become melancholy
70. that were much he should. It is unlikely he would do
    that.
71. no fear. nothing to fear

BRUTUS.
Peace! Count the clock.

CASSIUS.
      The clock hath stricken three.

TREBONIUS.
'Tis time to part.

CASSIUS.
      But it is doubtful yet
Whether Caesar will come forth today or no;
For he is superstitious grown of late,
Quite from the main opinion he held once [72]
Of fantasy, of dreams, and ceremonies. [73]
It may be these apparent prodigies, [74]
The unaccustomed terror of this night,
And the persuasion of his augurers [75]
May hold him from the Capitol today.

DECIUS.
Never fear that. If he be so resolved,
I can o'ersway him; for he loves to hear
That unicorns may be betrayed with trees, [76]

---

72. **from the main.** changed from the strong
73. **ceremonies.** omens
74. **apparent prodigies.** obvious strange happenings
75. **augurers.** officials who fortell the future by interpreting omens
76. **unicorns ... trees.** A story is told that a unicorn can be tricked into driving its horn into a tree if the hunter stands in front of the tree and steps aside at the correct moment as the unicorn charges.

And bears with glasses, elephants with holes, [77]
Lions with toils, and men with flatterers; [78]
But when I tell him he hates flatterers,
He says he does, being then most flattered.
Let me work;
For I can give his humor the true bent, [79]
And I will bring him to the Capitol.

CASSIUS.
Nay, we will all of us be there to fetch him.

BRUTUS.
By the eighth hour. Is that the uttermost? [80]

CINNA.
Be that the uttermost, and fail not then.

METELLUS.
Caius Ligarius doth bear Caesar hard, [81]
Who rated him for speaking well of Pompey. [82]
I wonder none of you have thought of him.

BRUTUS.
Now, good Metellus, go along by him. [83]
He loves me well, and I have given him reasons;
Send him but hither, and I'll fashion him. [84]

---

77. glasses. mirrors (allowing the hunter to approach the
   bear while it admires itself in the mirror)
   holes. pitfalls
78. toils. nets
79. give ... bent. change his disposition in the right direction
80. uttermost. latest
81. doth bear Caesar hard. has a grudge against Caesar
82. rated. berated, scolded
83. by him. by way of his house
84. fashion. persuade

CASSIUS.

The morning comes upon 's. we'll leave you, Brutus.
And, friends, disperse yourselves; but all remember
What you have said, and show yourselves true
    Romans.

BRUTUS.

Good gentlemen, look fresh and merrily;
Let not our looks put on our purposes, [85]
But bear it as our Roman actors do,
With untired spirits and formal constancy. [86]
And so good morrow to you every one.
                    [*Exit.* BRUTUS *remains*]
Boy! Lucius! Fast asleep? It is no matter.
Enjoy the honey-heavy dew of slumber.
Thou hast no figures nor no fantasies [87]
Which busy care draws in the brains of men;
Therefore thou sleep'st so sound.

[*Enter* PORTIA]

PORTIA.

                    Brutus, my lord!

BRUTUS.

Portia, what mean you? Wherefore rise you now?
It is not for your health thus to commit
Your weak condition to the raw cold morning.

PORTIA.

Nor for yours neither. You've ungently, Brutus, [88]

---

85. **put on.** show
86. **formal constancy.** consistent dignity
87. **figures.** imaginings
88. **ungently.** unkindly

Stole from my bed. And yesternight, at supper,
You suddenly arose, and walked about
Musing and sighing, with your arms across, [89]
And when I asked you what the matter was,
You stared upon me with ungentle looks.
I urged you further; then you scratched your head
And too impatiently stamped with your foot.
Yet I insisted, yet you answered not, [90]
But with an angry wafture of your hand [91]
Gave sign for me to leave you. So I did,
Fearing to strengthen that impatience
Which seemed too much enkindled, and withal [92]
Hoping it was but an effect of humor, [93]
Which sometimes hath his hour with every man. [94]
It will not let you eat, nor talk, nor sleep,
And could it work so much upon your shape
As it hath much prevailed on your condition, [95]
I should not know you Brutus. Dear my lord, [96]
Make me acquainted with your cause of grief.

BRUTUS.
I am not well in health, and that is all.

PORTIA.
Brutus is wise and, were he not in health,
He would embrace the means to come by it.

---

89. across. folded (a sign of sadness)
90. Yet ... yet. still ... still
91. wafture. waving
92. withal. indeed
93. humor. mood
94. his. its
95. condition. disposition
96. know you. recognize you as

BRUTUS.
Why, so I do. Good Portia, go to bed.

PORTIA.
Is Brutus sick? And is it physical [97]
To walk unbracèd and suck up the humors [98]
Of the dank morning? What, is Brutus sick,
And will he steal out of his wholesome bed
To dare the vile contagion of the night,
And tempt the rheumy and unpurgèd air [99]
To add unto his sickness? No, my Brutus,
You have some sick offense within your mind, [100]
Which by the right and virtue of my place
I ought to know of. [*She kneels*] And upon my knees
I charm you, by my once-commended beauty, [101]
By all your vows of love, and that great vow [102]
Which did incorporate and make us one,
That you unfold to me, your self, your half,
Why you are heavy, and what men tonight [103]
Have had resort to you; for here have been [104]
Some six or seven, who did hide their faces
Even from darkness.

---

97. **physical.** healthy
98. **unbracèd.** with loose clothing. **humors.** dampness
99. **rheumy ... air.** damp air that might cause
     rheumatism, a painful condition of the joints.
     unpurgèd. not purified by sunlight
100. **sick offense.** harmful sickness
101. **charm.** beg. **commended.** praised
102. **great vow.** marriage vow
103. **heavy.** sorrowful
104. **had resort to.** visited

BRUTUS.

Kneel not, gentle Portia.

[He raises her]

PORTIA.

I should not need if you were gentle Brutus.
Within the bond of marriage, tell me, Brutus,
Is it excepted I should know no secrets [105]
That appertain to you? Am I your self
But as it were in sort or limitation, [106]
To keep with you at meals, comfort your bed, [107]
And talk to you sometimes? Dwell I but in the
    suburbs [108]
Of your good pleasure? If it be no more,
Portia is Brutus' harlot, not his wife.

BRUTUS.

You are my true and honorable wife,
As dear to me as are the ruddy drops
That visit my sad heart.

PORTIA.

If this were true, then should I know this secret.
I grant I am a woman, but withal [109]
A woman that Lord Brutus took to wife.
I grant I am a woman, but withal

---

105. **excepted.** acceptable (that)
106. **in ... limitation.** only up to a point
107. **keep.** stay, be
108. **suburbs.** outskirts
109. **withal.** in addition

A woman well-reputed, Cato's daughter. [110]
Think you I am no stronger than my sex,
Being so fathered and so husbanded?
Tell me your counsels, I will not disclose 'em. [111]
I have made strong proof of my constancy,
Giving myself a voluntary wound
Here, in the thigh. Can I bear that with patience,
And not my husband's secrets?

BRUTUS.

O ye gods,
Render me worthy of this noble wife! [112]

[Knock within]

Hark, hark, one knocks. Portia, go in awhile,
And by and by thy bosom shall partake
The secrets of my heart.
All my engagements I will construe to thee, [113]
All the charactery of my sad brows. [114]
Leave me with haste.

[Exit PORTIA]

Lucius, who's that knocks?

[Enter LUCIUS *and* CAIUS LIGARIUS *wearing a kerchief]*

---

110. **Cato's daughter.** Marcus Porcius Cato sided with
     Pompey against Caesar in 48 B.C. He later killed
     himself rather than submit to Caesar's tyranny. He was
     Brutus' uncle as well as his father-in-law.
111. **counsels.** secrets
112. **Render.** make
113. **construe.** explain fully
114. **charactery ... brows.** all that is sad upon my face

LUCIUS.

Here is a sick man that would speak with you. [115]

BRUTUS.

Caius Ligarius, that Metellus spake of.
Boy, stand aside. [*Exit* LUCIUS] Caius Ligarius,
    how? [116]

LIGARIUS.

Vouchsafe good morrow from a feeble tongue.

BRUTUS.

O, what a time have you chose out, brave Caius, [117]
To wear a kerchief! would you were not sick!

LIGARIUS.

I am not sick, if Brutus have in hand
Any exploit worthy the name of honor.

BRUTUS.

Such an exploit have I in hand, Ligarius,
Had you a healthful ear to hear of it.

LIGARIUS.

By all the gods that Romans bow before,
I here discard my sickness! Soul of Rome!

[He throws off his kerchief]

---

115. **sick man.** In Elizabethan times a medicinal mixture
     was often applied to a cloth that was wrapped around
     the head of a patient.
116. **how.** how are you
117. **brave.** noble

Brave son, derived from honorable loins! [118]
Thou like an exorcist hast conjured up [119]
My mortifièd spirit. Now bid me run, [120]
And I will strive with things impossible,
Yea, get the better of them. What's to do?

BRUTUS.
A piece of work that will make sick men whole. [121]

LIGARIUS.
But are not some whole that we must make sick?

BRUTUS.
That must we also. What it is, my Caius,
I shall unfold to thee as we are going
To whom it must be done. [122]

LIGARIUS.
Set on your foot, [123]
And with a heart new-fired I follow you
To do I know not what; but it sufficeth [124]
That Brutus leads me on.

[Thunder]

BRUTUS.
Follow me, then.

[Exit]

---

118. **derived ... loins.** descended from Lucius Junius
    Brutus, founder of the Roman republic
119. **exorcist.** one who calls up spirits
120. **mortifièd.** deadened
121. **whole.** healthy
122. **To whom.** to him to whom
123. **Set on.** advance
124. **sufficeth.** is enough

---◆---

Synopsis of Act II, Scene 1

In the last scene, the conspirators met at Brutus's home at daybreak to make final plans for the murder. The conspirators agreed not to take a loyalty oath, not to include Cicero in their plot, and not to kill Mark Antony along with Caesar. Portia, Brutus's wife, pleaded with Brutus to tell her what was bothering him. Brutus was distracted by Caius Ligarius, another conspirator, but Brutus promised he would tell Portia his secrets.

---◆---

---◆---

Before You Read Act II, Scene 2

This scene begins a few hours later, in Caesar's house. Once again, the action takes place during a thunderstorm. Calpurnia, Caesar's wife, is asleep. In a dream, she calls out three times that Caesar is to be murdered. Calpurnia begs Caesar not to attend the Senate that day because he will be killed. Notice Caesar's attitude toward death. Once again, Caesar seems to be aware of what is happening, but does nothing about it. Caesar at first agrees to stay home and not attend the Senate. Notice how cleverly Decius changes Caesar's mind.

Brutus, Ligarius, and the other conspirators then enter Caesar's home. He invites them, along with Mark Antony who arrived late, to join him for wine. Notice Tribonius's promise to Caesar. How does Brutus once again reveal his noble nature as the scene closes?

---◆---

ACT II. Scene 2.

Location: Caesar's house.

[Thunder and lightning. Enter JULIUS CAESAR, in his dressing gown]

CAESAR.
Nor heaven nor earth have been at peace tonight. [1]
Thrice hath Calpurnia in her sleep cried out,
"Help, ho, they murder Caesar!" Who's within?

[Enter a SERVANT]

SERVANT.
My lord?

CAESAR.
Go bid the priests do present sacrifice [2]
And bring me their opinions of success. [3]

SERVANT.
I will, my lord.

[Exit]

[Enter CALPURNIA]

CALPURNIA.
What mean you, Caesar? Think you to walk forth?
You shall not stir out of your house today.

CAESAR.
Caesar shall forth. The things that threatened me [4]

---

1. **Nor.** neither
2. **present.** immediate.   **sacrifice.** pulling out the insides of sacrificed animals for omens
3. **opinions of success.** predictions for my success today
4. **forth.** go forth

Ne'er looked but on my back. When they shall see
The face of Caesar, they are vanishèd.

CALPURNIA.
Caesar, I never stood on ceremonies, [5]
Yet now they fright me. There is one within,
Besides the things that we have heard and seen,
Recounts most horrid sights seen by the watch. [6]
A lioness hath whelpèd in the streets, [7]
And graves have yawned and yielded up their dead. [8]
Fierce fiery warriors fight upon the clouds
In ranks and squadrons and right form of war, [9]
Which drizzled blood upon the Capitol.
The noise of battle hurtled in the air; [10]
Horses did neigh, and dying men did groan,
And ghosts did shriek and squeal about the streets.
O Caesar, these things are beyond all use, [11]
And I do fear them.

CAESAR.
                    What can be avoided
Whose end is purposed by the mighty gods? [12]

---

5. **stood on ceremonies.** paid attention to omens
6. **Recounts ... watch.** Tells about the awful sights seen
   by the watchman. (Watchmen existed in Elizabethan
   England, not in Rome.)
7. **whelpèd.** given birth
8. **yawned.** opened
9. **right form of war.** proper military formation
10. **hurtled.** clashed together
11. **beyond all use.** contrary to all experience
12. **is purposed.** is intended

Yet Caesar shall go forth; for these predictions
Are to the world in general as to Caesar. [13]

CALPURNIA.

When beggars die there are no comets seen;
The heavens themselves blaze forth the death of
    princes. [14]

CAESAR.

Cowards die many times before their deaths;
The valiant never taste of death but once.
Of all the wonders that I yet have heard,
It seems to me most strange that men should fear,
Seeing that death, a necessary end,
Will come when it will come.

[*Enter a* SERVANT]

                          What say the augurers?

SERVANT.

They would not have you to stir forth today.
Plucking the entrails of an offering forth,
They could not find a heart within the beast.

CAESAR.

The gods do this in shame of cowardice. [15]
Caesar should be a beast without a heart
If he should stay at home today for fear.
No, Caesar shall not. Danger knows full well
That Caesar is more dangerous than he.

---

13. **Are ... as to Caesar.** These predictions apply to the rest
    of the world as much as they apply to Caesar.
14. **blaze forth.** proclaim with meteors and comets
15. **in shame of.** in order to shame

We are two lions littered in one day,
And I the elder and more terrible?
And Caesar shall go forth.

CALPURNIA.

                   Alas, my lord,
Your wisdom is consumed in confidence. [16]
Do not go forth today! Call it my fear
That keeps you in the house, and not your own.
We'll send Mark Antony to the Senate House,
And he shall say you are not well today.
Let me, upon my knee, prevail in this.

                        [She kneels]

CAESAR.
Mark Antony shall say I am not well,
And for thy humor I will stay at home. [17]

                        [He raises her]

[Enter DECIUS]

Here's Decius Brutus. He shall tell them so.

DECIUS.
Caesar, all hail! Good morrow, worthy Caesar.
I come to fetch you to the Senate House.

CAESAR.
And you are come in very happy time [18]
To bear my greeting to the senators
And tell them that I will not come today.

---

16. **confidence.** overconfidence
17. **humor.** whim
18. **in very happy time.** at just the right moment

Cannot, is false, and that I dare not, falser;
I will not come today. Tell them so, Decius.

CALPURNIA.
Say he is sick.

CAESAR.
Shall Caesar send a lie?
Have I in conquest stretched mine arm so far
To be afeard to tell graybeards the truth? [19]
Decius, go tell them Caesar will not come.

DECIUS.
Most mighty Caesar, let me know some cause,
Lest I be laughed at when I tell them so.

CAESAR.
The cause is in my will: I will not come.
That is enough to satisfy the Senate.
But for your private satisfaction,
Because I love you, I will let you know.
Calpurnia here, my wife, stays me at home. [20]
She dreamt tonight she saw my statue,
Which like a fountain with an hundred spouts
Did run pure blood; and many lusty Romans [21]
Came smiling and did bathe their hands in it.
And these does she apply for warnings and
    portents [22]

---

19. **afeard to tell graybeards.** afraid to tell old men (the
    senators)
20. **stays.** detains
21. **lusty.** lively, merry
22. **apply for.** consider to be

And evils imminent, and on her knee
Hath begged that I will stay at home today.

DECIUS.
This dream is all amiss interpreted;
It was a vision fair and fortunate.
Your statue spouting blood in many pipes,
In which so many smiling Romans bathed,
Signifies that from you great Rome shall suck
Reviving blood, and that great men shall press [23]
For tinctures, stains, relics, and cognizance.
This by Calpurnia's dream is signified. [24]

CAESAR.
And this way have you well expounded it.

DECIUS.
I have, when you have heard what I can say;
And know it now. The Senate have concluded
To give this day a crown to mighty Caesar.
If you shall send them word you will not come,
Their minds may change. Besides, it were a mock [25]
Apt to be rendered for someone to say
"Break up the Senate till another time
When Caesar's wife shall meet with better dreams."
If Caesar hide himself, shall they not whisper
"Lo, Caesar is afraid"?

---

23. **press.** crowd around
24. **For ... signified.** Decius interprets Calpurnia's dream
    with a double meaning. To Caesar he suggests that
    people will beg for badges to show they are Caesar's
    servants; to the audience, that people will seek
    remembrances of his death.
25. **mock ... rendered.** jeering comment likely to be made

Pardon me, Caesar, for my dear dear love
To your proceeding bids me tell you this, [26]
And reason to my love is liable. [27]

CAESAR.
How foolish do your fears seem now, Calpurnia!
I am ashamèd I did yield to them.
Give me my robe, for I will go. [28]

[*Enter* BRUTUS, LIGARIUS, METELLUS,
CASCA, TREBONIUS, CINNA, *and* PUBLIUS]

And look where Publius is come to fetch me.

PUBLIUS.
Good morrow, Caesar.

CAESAR.
                                    Welcome, Publius.
What, Brutus, are you stirred so early too?
Good morrow, Casca. Caius Ligarius,
Caesar was ne'er so much your enemy
As that same ague which hath made you lean. [29]
What is 't o'clock?

BRUTUS.
                                    Caesar, 'tis strucken eight.

CAESAR.
I thank you for your pains and courtesy.

---

26. proceeding. advancing in your career
27. reason ... liable. my judgement is not as strong as my
    affection for you
28. robe. toga
29. ague. fever

[*Enter* ANTONY]

See, Antony, that revels long a' nights,
Is notwithstanding up. Good morrow, Antony.

ANTONY.
So to most noble Caesar.

CAESAR.
[*To a* SERVANT] Bid them prepare within. [30]

[*Exit* SERVANT]

I am to blame to be thus waited for.
Now, Cinna. Now, Metellus. What, Trebonius,
I have an hour's talk in store for you;
Remember that you call on me today.
Be near me, that I may remember you.

TREBONIUS.
Caesar, I will. [*Aside*] And so near will I be
That your best friends shall wish I had been further.

CAESAR.
Good friends, go in and taste some wine with me,
And we, like friends, will straightway go together.

BRUTUS.
[*Aside*]
That every like is not the same, O Caesar, [31]
The heart of Brutus earns to think upon! [32]

[*Exit*]

---

30. prepare within. set out food and wine
31. That ... same. that someone who seems to be a friend
    may be an enemy
32. earns. sorrows

---◆---

Synopsis of Act II, Scene 2

Caesar decided to attend the Senate even though his wife, Calpurnia, asked him not to go. At first he agreed and said he would not go. Then, when Decius told them that the senators would be offering Caesar the crown, he ignored her pleas and changed his mind. Decius also reinterpreted Calpurnia's dream in such a way as to tempt Caesar. Ironically, Caesar asked the senators to stay near him at the Senate.

---◆---

---◆---

Before You Read Act II, Scene 3

As Caesar walks toward the Capitol, Artemidorus, a traitor to the conspirators, is seen reading the conspirators' names from a paper. He says he will hand Caesar the paper as he goes to the Senate. Note what Artemidorus says about Caesar's carelessness. Do you think Caesar will read Artemidorus's note?

---◆---

ACT II. Scene 3.

Location: A street near the Capitol.

[*Enter* ARTEMIDORUS *reading a paper*]

ARTEMIDORUS..

"Caesar, beware of Brutus; take heed of Cassius;
come not near Casca; have an eye to Cinna; trust
not Trebonius; mark well Metellus Cimber; Decius
Brutus loves thee not; thou hast wronged Caius
Ligarius. There is but one mind in all these men,
and it is bent [1] against Caesar. If thou beest not
immortal, look about you. Security [2] gives way to
conspiracy. [3] The mighty gods defend thee!
                    Thy lover, Artemidorus." [4]
Here will I stand till Caesar pass along,
And as a suitor will I give him this. [5]
My heart laments that virtue cannot live
Out of the teeth of emulation. [6]
If thou read this, O Caesar, thou mayest live;
If not, the Fates with traitors do contrive. [7]
                                        [*Exit*]

---

1. **bent.** directed
2. **Security.** overconfidence
3. **gives ... conspiracy.** allows the conspiracy to proceed
4. **lover.** friend
5. **suitor.** person who makes requests or petitions
6. **Out ... emulation.** beyond the reach of envy
7. **contrive.** conspire

---◆---

Synopsis of Act II, Scene 3

In the previous scene, Artemidorus was standing on the street, near the Capitol, reading a list of conspirators' names. He knew, not only their names, but the details of the plot. Artemidorus said he would hand the paper to Caesar.

---◆---

---◆---

Before You Read Act II, Scene 4

While Artemidorus waits for Caesar, Portia sends their servant, Lucius, to find out what is happening at the Capitol. The soothsayer enters. Notice what Portia asks him. Since the date is March 15th, what might the soothsayer want to tell Caesar? What does Portia say that tells she is fully aware of the details of the plot?

---◆---

ACT II. Scene 4.

Location: Before the house of Brutus.

[*Enter* PORTIA *and* LUCIUS]

PORTIA.
I prithee, boy, run to the Senate House.
Stay not to answer me, but get thee gone.
Why dost thou stay?

LUCIUS.
To know my errand, madam.

PORTIA.
I would have had thee there and here again
Ere I can tell thee what thou shouldst do there.
[*Aside*] O constancy, be strong upon my side; [1]
Set a huge mountain 'tween my heart and tongue!
I have a man's mind, but a woman's might.
How hard it is for women to keep counsel! [2]
Art thou here yet?

LUCIUS.
Madam, what should I do?
Run to the Capitol, and nothing else?
And so return to you, and nothing else?

PORTIA.
Yes, bring me word, boy, if thy lord look well,
For he went sickly forth; and take good note [3]

---

1. **constancy.** firmness of mind or purpose
2. **counsel.** a secret
3. **take good note.** watch closely

What Caesar doth, what suitors press to him.
Hark, boy, what noise is that?

LUCIUS.
I hear none, madam.

PORTIA.
                    Prithee, listen well.
I heard a bustling rumor, like a fray, [4]
And the wind brings it from the Capitol.

LUCIUS.
Sooth, madam, I hear nothing. [5]

[*Enter the* SOOTHSAYER]

PORTIA.
Come hither, fellow. Which way hast thou been?

SOOTHSAYER.
At mine own house, good lady.

PORTIA.
What is 't o'clock?

SOOTHSAYER.
                    About the ninth hour, lady.

PORTIA.
Is Caesar yet gone to the Capitol?

SOOTHSAYER.
Madam, not yet. I go to take my stand,
To see him pass on to the Capitol.

---

4. **bustling rumor.** confused sound.   **fray.** brawl
5. **Sooth.** surely

PORTIA.
Thou hast some suit to Caesar, hast thou not? [6]

SOOTHSAYER.
That I have, lady, if it will please Caesar
To be so good to Caesar as to hear me:
I shall beseech him to befriend himself.

PORTIA.
Why, know'st thou any harms intended towards
him?

SOOTHSAYER.
None that I know will be, much that I fear may
chance.
Good morrow to you. Here the street is narrow.
The throng that follows Caesar at the heels,
Of senators, of praetors, common suitors, [7]
Will crowd a feeble man almost to death.
I'll get me to a place more void, and there [8]
Speak to great Caesar as he comes along.
[*Exit*]

PORTIA.
I must go in. Ay me, how weak a thing
The heart of woman is! O Brutus,
The heavens speed thee in thine enterprise!
Sure, the boy heard me. — Brutus hath a suit
That Caesar will not grant. — O, I grow faint. —

---

6. **suit.** petition
7. **praetors.** judges
8. **void.** empty, uncrowded

Run, Lucius, and commend me to my lord;
Say I am merry. Come to me again
And bring me word what he doth say to thee.

[*Exit separately*]

---◆---

Synopsis of Act II, Scene 4

Suspense continued to build in the play as Portia sent Lucius to find out what Brutus and Caesar were doing at the Capitol. Then the soothsayer entered and said that he wanted to speak with Caesar. Portia found out that the soothsayer did not know about the conspiracy. Portia was clearly worried about her husband.

---◆---

———————◆———————

Before You Read Act III, Scene 1

At the beginning of this scene, Caesar is given two more chances to save himself from the conspiracy. Notice how he reacts when he sees the soothsayer. Pay attention to what happens when Artemidorus hands Caesar the note with the conspirators' names.

The procession moves to the Senate chamber. Notice how the senators get Caesar's attention. Think about Caesar's response to Metellus's request. This response tells you something about how Caesar views his power.

The senators attack Caesar. Notice what Caesar says when he sees that Brutus has betrayed him. Caesar dies and the conspirators discover that they should have planned more carefully.

Antony flees to his house, but he sends a servant to the conspirators to find out how he will be treated. Notice how Brutus's words about Mark Antony contrast with what Cassius says. Mark Antony enters and says that if they are going to kill him to do so now. Brutus assures Antony he will not be killed. Notice what Brutus says to Antony about the feelings of the conspirators.

Antony begins a speech in praise of Caesar, but Cassius interrupts to ask if he will support them, or if they should proceed without him. Pay attention to how Antony responds to Cassius. Cassius says something that shows he is beginning to suspect Antony's intentions. What does he fear will happen if Mark Antony speaks to the people? Brutus gives Antony five conditions under which he may speak. What are they?

Mark Antony, now alone with Caesar's body, gives an eloquent speech. What does Antony say he will do? As the scene closes, a servant enters and says that his master, Octavius, whom Caesar had summoned to Rome, has arrived. What warning does Antony send back to Octavius?

———————◆———————

ACT III. Scene 1.

Location: Before the Capitol.

[*Flourish of trumpets. Enter* CAESAR, BRUTUS,
CASSIUS, CASCA, DECIUS, METELLUS
CIMBER, TREBONIUS, CINNA, ANTONY,
LEPIDUS, ARTEMIDORUS, PUBLIUS,
POPILIUS LENA, *and the* SOOTHSAYER; *others
following*]

CAESAR.
[*To the* SOOTHSAYER]
The ides of March are come.

SOOTHSAYER.
Ay, Caesar, but not gone.

ARTEMIDORUS.
Hail, Caesar! Read this schedule. [1]

DECIUS.
Trebonius doth desire you to o'erread, [2]
At your best leisure, this his humble suit.

ARTEMIDORUS.
O Caesar, read mine first, for mine's a suit
That touches Caesar nearer. Read it, great Caesar.

CAESAR.
What touches us ourself shall be last served.

---

1. **schedule.** paper
2. **o'erread.** read over thoroughly

ARTEMIDORUS.
Delay not, Caesar, read it instantly.

CAESAR.
What, is the fellow mad?

PUBLIUS.
Sirrah, give place. [3]

CASSIUS.
What, urge you your petitions in the street?
Come to the Capitol.

[CAESAR *goes to the Capitol and takes his place,*
the rest following]

POPILIUS.
[*To* CASSIUS]
I wish your enterprise today may thrive.

CASSIUS.
What enterprise, Popilius?

POPILIUS.
Fare you well.

[*He advances to* CAESAR]

BRUTUS.
What said Popilius Lena?

CASSIUS.
He wished today our enterprise might thrive.
I fear our purpose is discoverèd.

---

3. **Sirrah.** fellow. (an address made to people of lesser
    social rank). **give place.** get out of the way

BRUTUS.

Look how he makes to Caesar. Mark him. [4]

[POPILIUS *speaks apart to* CAESAR]

CASSIUS.

Casca, be sudden, for we fear prevention. [5]
Brutus, what shall be done? If this be known,
Cassius or Caesar never shall turn back, [6]
For I will slay myself.

BRUTUS.

Cassius, be constant. [7]
Popilius Lena speaks not of our purposes;
For look, he smiles, and Caesar doth not change. [8]

CASSIUS.

Trebonius knows his time, for look you, Brutus,
He draws Mark Antony out of the way.

[*Exit* TREBONIUS *with* ANTONY]

DECIUS.

Where is Metellus Cimber? Let him go
And presently prefer his suit to Caesar. [9]

BRUTUS.

He is addressed. Press near and second him. [10]

---

4. makes to. approaches
5. sudden. quick.   **prevention.** being forestalled
6. turn back. return alive
7. constant. firm
8. Caesar ... change. Caesar's expression does not change.
9. presently ... his suit. immediately present his petition
10. addressed. ready.   **second.** support

CINNA.

Casca, you are the first that rears your hand.

[*They press near* CAESAR]

CAESAR.

Are we all ready? What is now amiss
That Caesar and his Senate must redress?

METELLUS.

[*Kneeling*]

Most high, most mighty, and most puissant Caesar, [11]
Metellus Cimber throws before thy seat
An humble heart —

CAESAR.

I must prevent thee, Cimber. [12]
These couchings and these lowly courtesies [13]
Might fire the blood of ordinary men, [14]
And turn preordinance and first decree [15]
Into the law of children. Be not fond [16]
To think that Caesar bears such rebel blood
That will be thawed from the true quality [17]
With that which melteth fools — I mean, sweet
    words,

---

11. **puissant.** powerful
12. **prevent.** forestall
13. **couchings ... lowly courtesies.** bows and humble
    gestures of reverence
14. **fire the blood of.** incite
15. **And turn ... of children.** and change what has already
    been decided, as children might change their minds
16. **fond.** foolish
17. **rebel blood ... quality.** an unstable disposition that will
    be changed from firmness

Low-crookèd curtsies, and base spaniel fawning. [18]
Thy brother by decree is banishèd.
If thou dost bend and pray and fawn for him, [19]
I spurn thee like a cur out of my way. [20]
Know, Caesar doth not wrong, nor without cause
Will he be satisfied.

METELLUS.
Is there no voice more worthy than my own
To sound more sweetly in great Caesar's ear
For the repealing of my banished brother? [21]

BRUTUS.

[Kneeling]
I kiss thy hand, but not in flattery, Caesar,
Desiring thee that Publius Cimber may
Have an immediate freedom of repeal. [22]

CAESAR.
What, Brutus?

CASSIUS.

[Kneeling]
Pardon, Caesar! Caesar, pardon!
As low as to thy foot doth Cassius fall,
To beg enfranchisement for Publius Cimber. [23]

---

18. **Low-crookèd.** deep. **base spaniel fawning.** low,
    dog-like cringing
19. **bend.** bow
20. **spurn.** kick. **cur.** dog of mixed breed
21. **repealing.** recall
22. **freedom of repeal.** permission to be recalled
23. **enfranchisement.** freedom from the decree of
    banishment

CAESAR.

I could be well moved, if I were as you;
If I could pray to move, prayers would move me. [24]
But I am constant as the northern star,
Of whose true-fixed and resting quality [25]
There is no fellow in the firmament. [26]
The skies are painted with unnumbered sparks;
They are all fire and every one doth shine;
But there's but one in all doth hold his place. [27]
So in the world: 'tis furnished well with men,
And men are flesh and blood, and apprehensive; [28]
Yet in the number I do know but one
That unassailable holds on his rank, [29]
Unshaked of motion. And that I am he, [30]
Let me a little show it even in this —
That I was constant Cimber should be banished,
And constant do remain to keep him so.

CINNA.

[*Kneeling*]

O Caesar —

CAESAR.

Hence! Wilt thou lift up Olympus? [31]

---

24. **pray to move.** ask others to change their mind
25. **true-fixed.** unmovable. **resting.** unchanging
26. **fellow.** equal. **firmament.** sky
27. **his.** its
28. **apprehensive.** able to understand
29. **rank.** position
30. **Unshaked of motion.** unmoved by his own or others' actions
31. **Olympus.** a mountain in northern Greece that was, in Greek mythology, the home of the gods (Caesar compares himself to the mountain which cannot move and the gods who remain aloof.)

DECIUS.

[*Kneeling*]

Great Caesar —

CAESAR.

Doth not Brutus bootless kneel? [32]

CASCA.

Speak, hands, for me!

[*They stab* CAESAR, CASCA *first,* BRUTUS *last*].

CAESAR.

Et tu, Brutè? Then fall, Caesar! [33]

[*Dies*]

CINNA.

Liberty! Freedom! Tyranny is dead!
Run hence, proclaim, cry it about the streets.

CASSIUS.

Some to the common pulpits, and cry out [34]
"Liberty, freedom, and enfranchisement!"

BRUTUS.

People and senators, be not affrighted.
Fly not; stand still. Ambition's debt is paid. [35]

CASCA.

Go to the pulpit, Brutus.

DECIUS.

And Cassius too.

---

32. **bootless.** uselessly
33. **Et tu, Brutè.** and thou, Brutus
34. **common pulpits.** speakers' platforms
35. **Ambition's ... paid.** ambition received what it deserved

BRUTUS.
Where's Publius? [36]

CINNA.
Here, quite confounded with this mutiny. [37]

METELLUS.
Stand fast together, lest some friend of Caesar's
Should chance —

BRUTUS.
Talk not of standing. — Publius, good cheer. [38]
There is no harm intended to your person,
Nor to no Roman else. So tell them, Publius.

CASSIUS.
And leave us, Publius, lest that the people,
Rushing on us, should do your age some mischief.

BRUTUS.
Do so, and let no man abide this deed [39]
But we the doers.
                    [*Exit all but the conspirators*]

[*Enter* TREBONIUS]

CASSIUS.
Where is Antony?

TREBONIUS.
                    Fled to his house amazed. [40]

---

36. Publius. An old senator, too confused to flee
37. mutiny. uprising
38. standing. resistance
39. let no man abide. let no man take responsibility for
40. amazed. astounded

Men, wives, and children stare, cry out, and run
As it were doomsday. [41]

BRUTUS.

                Fates, we will know your
   pleasures.
That we shall die, we know; 'tis but the time,
And drawing days out, that men stand upon. [42]

CASCA.

Why, he that cuts off twenty years of life
Cuts off so many years of fearing death.

BRUTUS.

Grant that, and then is death a benefit.
So are we Caesar's friends, that have abridged
His time of fearing death. Stoop, Romans, stoop,
And let us bathe our hands in Caesar's blood
Up to the elbows and besmear our swords.
Then walk we forth even to the marketplace, [43]
And, waving our red weapons o'er our heads,
Let's all cry "Peace, freedom, and liberty!"

CASSIUS.

Stoop, then, and wash. [*They bathe their hands
   and weapons*] How many ages hence
Shall this our lofty scene be acted over
In states unborn and accents yet unknown! [44]

---

41. As. as if
42. drawing ... upon. prolonging life that people care about
43. the marketplace. the Forum
44. accents. languages

BRUTUS.
How many times shall Caesar bleed in sport, [45]
That now on Pompey's basis lies along [46]
No worthier than the dust!

CASSIUS.
                So oft as that shall be,
So often shall the knot of us be called [47]
The men that gave their country liberty.

DECIUS.
What, shall we forth?

CASSIUS.
              Ay, every man away.
Brutus shall lead, and we will grace his heels [48]
With the most boldest and best hearts of Rome.

[*Enter a* SERVANT]

BRUTUS.
Soft, who comes here? A friend of Antony's.

SERVANT.
    [*Kneeling*]
Thus, Brutus, did my master bid me kneel;
Thus did Mark Antony bid me fall down,
And being prostrate, thus he bade me say:
"Brutus is noble, wise, valiant, and honest;

---

45. **in sport.** in plays
46. **on Pompey's ... along.** by the pedestal of Pompey's
    statue lies stretched out
47. **knot.** group
48. **grace his heels.** honor him by following him

Caesar was mighty, bold, royal, and loving.
Say I love Brutus and I honor him;
Say I feared Caesar, honored him, and loved him.
If Brutus will vouchsafe that Antony [49]
May safely come to him and be resolved [50]
How Caesar hath deserved to lie in death,
Mark Antony shall not love Caesar dead
So well as Brutus living, but will follow
The fortunes and affairs of noble Brutus
Thorough the hazards of this untrod state [51]
With all true faith." So says my master Antony.

BRUTUS.
Thy master is a wise and valiant Roman;
I never thought him worse.
Tell him, so please him come unto this place, [52]
He shall be satisfied and, by my honor,
Depart untouched.

SERVANT.
                I'll fetch him presently. [53]

                    [*Exit* SERVANT]

BRUTUS.
I know that we shall have him well to friend. [54]

CASSIUS.
I wish we may. But yet have I a mind

---

49. **vouchsafe.** allow
50. **be resolved.** have it explained
51. **Thorough.** through.   **untrod state.** new state of affairs
52. **so.** if it should
53. **presently.** immediately
54. **to friend.** as a friend

That fears him much, and my misgiving still [55]
Falls shrewdly to the purpose.

[*Enter* ANTONY]

BRUTUS.
But here comes Antony. Welcome, Mark Antony.

ANTONY.
O mighty Caesar! Dost thou lie so low?
Are all thy conquests, glories, triumphs, spoils,
Shrunk to this little measure? Fare thee well. —
I know not, gentlemen, what you intend,
Who else must be let blood, who else is rank; [56]
If I myself, there is no hour so fit
As Caesar's death's hour, nor no instrument
Of half that worth as those your swords, made rich
With the most noble blood of all this world.
I do beseech ye, if you bear me hard, [57]
Now, whilst your purpled hands do reek and smoke, [58]
Fulfill your pleasure. Live a thousand years, [59]
I shall not find myself so apt to die; [60]
No place will please me so, no means of death,
As here by Caesar, and by you cut off,
The choice and master spirits of this age.

---

55. **fears.** distrusts.   **my misgiving still ... purpose.** my
instincts are usually accurate
56. **let blood.** killed.   **rank.** diseased and in need of
bloodletting
57. **bear me hard.** have a grudge against me
58. **purpled.** bloody.   **reek.** steam
59. **Live.** if I should live
60. **apt.** ready

BRUTUS.

O Antony! Beg not your death of us.
Though now we must appear bloody and cruel,
As by our hands and this our present act
You see we do, yet see you but our hands
And this the bleeding business they have done.
Our hearts you see not. They are pitiful; [61]
And pity to the general wrong of Rome —
As fire drives out fire, so pity pity — [62]
Hath done this deed on Caesar. For your part,
To you our swords have leaden points, Mark
    Antony. [63]
Our arms in strength of malice, and our hearts
Of brothers' temper, do receive you in [64]
With all kind love, good thoughts, and reverence.

CASSIUS.

Your voice shall be as strong as any man's [65]
In the disposing of new dignities. [66]

BRUTUS.

Only be patient till we have appeased
The multitude, beside themselves with fear,
And then we will deliver you the cause [67]
Why I, that did love Caesar when I struck him,
Have thus proceeded.

---

61. **pitiful.** full of pity
62. **pity pity.** pity for Rome drove out pity for Caesar
63. **leaden.** blunt, dull
64. **Of brothers' temper.** full of brotherly feeling
65. **voice.** vote, authority
66. **dignities.** offices of state
67. **deliver.** tell to

ANTONY.

                          I doubt not of your wisdom.
Let each man render me his bloody hand.

        [He shakes hands with the conspirators]

First, Marcus Brutus, will I shake with you;
Next, Caius Cassius, do I take your hand;
Now, Decius Brutus, yours; now yours, Metellus;
Yours, Cinna; and, my valiant Casca, yours;
Though last, not least in love, yours, good Trebonius.
Gentlemen all — alas, what shall I say?
My credit now stands on such slippery ground [68]
That one of two bad ways you must conceit me, [69]
Either a coward or a flatterer.
That I did love thee, Caesar, O, 'tis true!
If then thy spirit look upon us now,
Shall it not grieve thee dearer than thy death [70]
To see thy Antony making his peace,
Shaking the bloody fingers of thy foes —
Most noble! — in the presence of thy corpse?
Had I as many eyes as thou hast wounds,
Weeping as fast as they stream forth thy blood,
It would become me better than to close [71]
In terms of friendship with thine enemies.
Pardon me, Julius! Here wast thou bayed, brave
    hart; [72]
Here didst thou fall, and here thy hunters stand,

---

68. credit. reputation
69. conceit. think of
70. dearer. more deeply
71. close. to reach an agreement
72. bayed. cornered. **hart.** deer

Signed in thy spoil and crimsoned in thy lethe. [73]
O world, thou wast the forest to this hart,
And this indeed, O world, the heart of thee!
How like a deer, strucken by many princes, [74]
Dost thou here lie!

CASSIUS.
Mark Antony —

ANTONY.
Pardon me, Caius Cassius.
The enemies of Caesar shall say this; [75]
Then in a friend it is cold modesty. [76]

CASSIUS.
I blame you not for praising Caesar so,
But what compact mean you to have with us? [77]
Will you be pricked in number of our friends, [78]
Or shall we on and not depend on you? [79]

ANTONY.
Therefore I took your hands, but was indeed
Swayed from the point by looking down on Caesar.
Friends am I with you all, and love you all,
Upon this hope, that you shall give me reasons
Why and wherein Caesar was dangerous.

---

73. **Signed ... spoil.** marked with the signs of your
slaughter. **lethe.** river of blood
74. **strucken.** struck down
75. **The enemies.** even the enemies
76. **cold.** calm. **modesty.** moderate speech
77. **compact.** agreement
78. **pricked in number.** marked off on a list
79. **on.** proceed

BRUTUS.
Or else were this a savage spectacle. [80]
Our reasons are so full of good regard [81]
That were you, Antony, the son of Caesar,
You should be satisfied.

ANTONY.
That's all I seek,
And am moreover suitor that I may
Produce his body to the marketplace, [82]
And in the pulpit, as becomes a friend, [83]
Speak in the order of his funeral. [84]

BRUTUS.
You shall, Mark Antony.

CASSIUS.
Brutus, a word with you.
[*Aside* to BRUTUS] You know not what you do. Do
not consent
That Antony speak in his funeral.
Know you how much the people may be moved
By that which he will utter?

BRUTUS.
[*Aside to* CASSIUS] By your pardon:
I will myself into the pulpit first
And show the reason of our Caesar's death.

---

80. **else were this.** otherwise this would be
81. **so ... regard.** so carefully considered
82. **Produce.** bring forth
83. **pulpit.** public platform
84. **order.** ceremony

What Antony shall speak, I will protest [85]
He speaks by leave and by permission,
And that we are contented Caesar shall
Have all true rites and lawful ceremonies.
It shall advantage more than do us wrong.

CASSIUS.
    [*Aside to* BRUTUS]
    I know not what may fall. I like it not. [86]

BRUTUS.
    Mark Antony, here, take you Caesar's body.
    You shall not in your funeral speech blame us,
    But speak all good you can devise of Caesar,
    And say you do 't by our permission.
    Else shall you not have any hand at all
    About his funeral. And you shall speak
    In the same pulpit whereto I am going,
    After my speech is ended.

ANTONY.
                        Be it so.
    I do desire no more.

BRUTUS.
    Prepare the body then, and follow us.

                        [*Exit.* ANTONY *remains*]

ANTONY.
    O, pardon me, thou bleeding piece of earth,
    That I am meek and gentle with these butchers!

---

85. protest. announce
86. fall. happen

Thou are the ruins of the noblest man
That ever livèd in the tide of times. [87]
Woe to the hand that shed this costly blood! [88]
Over thy wounds now do I prophesy —
Which, like dumb mouths, do ope their ruby lips
To beg the voice and utterance of my tongue —
A curse shall light upon the limbs of men;
Domestic fury and fierce civil strife
Shall cumber all the parts of Italy; [89]
Blood and destruction shall be so in use
And dreadful objects so familiar [90]
That mothers shall but smile when they behold
Their infants quartered with the hands of war, [91]
All pity choked with custom of fell deeds; [92]
And Caesar's spirit, ranging for revenge, [93]
With Ate by his side come hot from hell, [94]
Shall in these confines with a monarch's voice [95]
Cry "Havoc!" and let slip the dogs of war, [96]
That this foul deed shall smell above the earth [97]
With carrion men, groaning for burial.

[*Enter* OCTAVIUS' SERVANT]

---

87. tide of times. course of all history
88. costly. valuable (in that it led to dire consequences)
89. cumber. burden
90. objects. sights
91. quartered. cut to pieces
92. custom ... deeds. the familiarity of cruel deeds
93. ranging. roaming like a wild beast in search of prey
94. Ate. Greek goddess of discord and moral chaos
95. confines. boundaries
96. Havoc. the signal to begin general slaughter.
    let slip. set loose
97. That. so that

You serve Octavius Caesar, do you not?

SERVANT.
I do, Mark Antony.

ANTONY.
Caesar did write for him to come to Rome.

SERVANT.
He did receive his letters, and is coming,
And bid me say to you by word of mouth —
O Caesar!

[*Seeing the body*]

ANTONY.
Thy heart is big. Get thee apart and weep. [98]
Passion, I see, is catching, for mine eyes,
Seeing those beads of sorrow stand in thine,
Began to water. Is thy master coming?

SERVANT.
He lies tonight within seven leagues of Rome. [99]

ANTONY.
Post back with speed and tell him what hath
    chanced.
Here is a mourning Rome, a dangerous Rome,
No Rome of safety for Octavius yet;
Hie hence and tell him so. Yet stay awhile; [100]
Thou shalt not back till I have borne this corpse

---

98. big. filled with grief
99. lies ... seven leagues. is camped tonight within 21 miles
100. Hie. hasten

Into the marketplace. There shall I try, [101]
In my oration, how the people take
The cruel issue of these bloody men, [102]
According to the which thou shalt discourse [103]
To young Octavius of the state of things. [104]
Lend me your hand.

                    [*Exit with* CAESAR'S *body*]

---

101. try. test
102. issue. deed
103. the which. the outcome of which
104. young Octavius. He was eighteen in March of 44 B.C.

---◆---

Synopsis of Act III, Scene 1

Act III, Scene 1, was the turning point in the
play. In this scene, Caesar went to the Capitol and
ignored his two last chances to alter fate. The
conspirators surrounded Caesar in the Capitol, as
if protesting his decision to uphold banishment of
Metellus Cimber's brother. Casca stabbed Caesar
first. Upon seeing Brutus among the conspirators,
Caesar gave in and did not resist. The conspirators
had not made a plan for what to do after killing
Caesar and there was total chaos among the
senators. Mark Antony arrived and, after being
assured that he would not be killed, asked to speak
at Caesar's funeral. Brutus agreed that Antony
could speak but only under five specific conditions.
Octavius, Caesar's nephew, arrived, but Antony
warned him not to enter the city because "Rome is
dangerous."

---◆---

----◆----

Before You Read Act III, Scene 2

The funeral takes place at the forum and the plebeians, or common people, arrive to hear Antony and Brutus speak. Notice what explanation Brutus gives for killing Caesar, even though he loved him. Antony enters, carrying Caesar's body. Brutus says that, if necessary, he too will die for Rome. Pay attention to how the crowd responds to Brutus's words. Antony's funeral oration, one of the most important speeches in the play, begins in a calm tone. Antony tells the people of Rome that he has come to bury Caesar, not to praise him. Notice that he refers to Brutus as an honorable man. Antony takes out Caesar's will and the people beg to hear it. Antony tells the people he will read the will after they form a ring, or circle, around Caesar's body. Then Antony describes the murder in detail and points to the stab wounds in Caesar's mutilated body. Notice how Antony uses words to sway the crowd. Pay attention to how Antony incites the Roman people into a rage. What has Caesar left to every Roman citizen? Note Mark Antony's words that show his satisfaction with the crowd's reaction.

----◆----

ACT III. Scene 2.

Location: The Forum.

[Enter BRUTUS *and presently goes into the pulpit, and* CASSIUS, *with the* PLEBEIANS] [1]

PLEBEIANS.
We will be satisfied! Let us be satisfied! [2]

BRUTUS.
Then follow me, and give me audience, friends.
Cassius, go you into the other street
And part the numbers. [3]
Those that will hear me speak, let 'em stay here;
Those that will follow Cassius, go with him;
And public reasons shall be renderèd
Of Caesar's death.

FIRST PLEBEIAN.
                    I will hear Brutus speak.

SECOND PLEBEIAN.
I will hear Cassius, and compare their reasons
When severally [4] we hear them renderèd.

[Exit CASSIUS, *with some of the* PLEBEIANS]

THIRD PLEBEIAN.
The noble Brutus is ascended. Silence!

---

1. **Plebeians.** commoners or members of the lower class
2. **be satisfied.** have an explanation
3. **part the numbers.** divide the crowd
4. **severally.** separately

BRUTUS.

Be patient till the last. Romans, countrymen, and lovers, [5] hear me for my cause, and be silent that you may hear. Believe me for mine honor, and have respect to mine honor, that you may believe. Censure [6] me in your wisdom, and awake your senses, that you may the better judge. If there be any in this assembly, any dear friend of Caesar's, to him I say that Brutus' love to Caesar was no less than his. If then that friend demand why Brutus rose against Caesar, this is my answer: not that I loved Caesar less, but that I loved Rome more. Had you rather Caesar were living and die all slaves, than that Caesar were dead, to live all free men? As Caesar loved me, I weep for him; as he was fortunate, I rejoice at it; as he was valiant, I honor him; but, as he was ambitious, I slew him. There is tears for his love; joy for his fortune; honor for his valor; and death for his ambition. Who is here so base that would be a bondman? If any, speak, for him have I offended. Who is here so rude [7] that would not be a Roman? If any, speak, for him have I offended. Who is here so vile that will not love his country? If any, speak, for him have I offended. I pause for a reply.

ALL.

None, Brutus, none!

---

5. **lovers.** friends
6. **Censure.** condemn as wrong
7. **rude.** ignorant

BRUTUS.
Then none have I offended. I have done no more to
Caesar than you shall [8] do to Brutus. The question
of his death is enrolled [9] in the Capitol, his glory
not extenuated [10] wherein he was worthy, nor his
offenses enforced [11] for which he suffered death.

[*Enter* MARK ANTONY *and others with*
CAESAR'S *body*]

Here comes his body, mourned by Mark Antony,
who, though he had no hand in his death, shall
receive the benefit of his dying, a place in the
commonwealth, as which of you shall not? With
this I depart, that, as I slew my best lover [12] for the
good of Rome, I have the same dagger for myself
when it shall please my country to need my death.

ALL.
Live, Brutus, live, live!

[BRUTUS *comes down*]

FIRST PLEBEIAN.
Bring him with triumph home unto his house.

SECOND PLEBEIAN.
Give him a statue with his ancestors.

---

8. shall. should
9. The question ... enrolled. The entire matter of
Caesar's death is on record at the Capitol.
10. extenuated. belittled
11. enforced. overemphasized
12. lover. friend

THIRD PLEBEIAN.
Let him be Caesar.

FOURTH PLEBEIAN.
Caesar's better parts
Shall be crowned in Brutus.

FIRST PLEBEIAN.
We'll bring him to his house with shouts and
clamors.

BRUTUS.
My countrymen —

SECOND PLEBEIAN.
Peace, silence! Brutus speaks.

FIRST PLEBEIAN.
Peace, ho!

BRUTUS.
Good countrymen, let me depart alone,
And, for my sake, stay here with Antony.
Do grace to Caesar's corpse, and grace his speech [13]
Tending to Caesar's glories, which Mark Antony, [14]
By our permission, is allowed to make.
I do entreat you, not a man depart,
Save I alone, till Antony have spoke.

[Exit]

---

13. **Do grace.** show respect.   **grace his speech.** listen
courteously to Antony's speech
14. **Tending to.** dealing with

FIRST PLEBEIAN.
Stay, ho, and let us hear Mark Antony.

THIRD PLEBEIAN.
Let him go up into the public chair.
We'll hear him. Noble Antony, go up.

ANTONY.
For Brutus' sake I am beholding to you. ¹⁵

[*He goes into the pulpit*]

FOURTH PLEBEIAN.
What does he say of Brutus?

THIRD PLEBEIAN.
He says, for Brutus' sake
He finds himself beholding to us all.

FOURTH PLEBEIAN.
'Twere best he speak no harm of Brutus here.

FIRST PLEBEIAN.
This Caesar was a tyrant.

THIRD PLEBEIAN.
Nay, that's certain
We are blest that Rome is rid of him.

SECOND PLEBEIAN.
Peace! Let us hear what Antony can say.

ANTONY.
You gentle Romans —

---

15. beholding. indebted

ALL.

Peace, ho! Let us hear him.

ANTONY.

Friends, Romans, countrymen, lend me your ears. [16]
I come to bury Caesar, not to praise him.
The evil that men do lives after them;
The good is oft interrèd with their bones.
So let it be with Caesar. The noble Brutus
Hath told you Caesar was ambitious.
If it were so, it was a grievous fault,
And grievously hath Caesar answered it. [17]
Here, under leave of Brutus and the rest [18]
(For Brutus is an honorable man,
So are they all, all honorable men)
Come I to speak in Caesar's funeral.
He was my friend, faithful and just to me;
But Brutus says he was ambitious,
And Brutus is an honorable man.
He hath brought many captives home to Rome.
Whose ransoms did the general coffers fill.
Did this in Caesar seem ambitious?
When that the poor have cried, Caesar hath wept;
Ambition should be made of sterner stuff.
Yet Brutus says he was ambitious,
And Brutus is an honorable man.
You all did see that on the Lupercal
I thrice presented him a kingly crown,
Which he did thrice refuse. Was this ambition?

---

16. **lend ... ears.** listen to me
17. **answered.** paid for
18. **under leave.** by permission

Yet Brutus says he was ambitious,
And sure he is an honorable man.
I speak not to disprove what Brutus spoke,
But here I am to speak what I do know.
You all did love him once, not without cause.
What cause withholds you then to mourn for him?
O judgment! Thou art fled to brutish beasts,
And men have lost their reason. Bear with me;
My heart is in the coffin there with Caesar,
And I must pause till it come back to me.

FIRST PLEBEIAN.
Methinks there is much reason in his sayings.

SECOND PLEBEIAN.
If thou consider rightly of the matter,
Caesar has had great wrong.

THIRD PLEBEIAN.
                              Has he, masters?
I fear there will a worse come in his place.

FOURTH PLEBEIAN.
Marked ye his words? He would not take the
   crown,
Therefore 'tis certain he was not ambitious.

FIRST PLEBEIAN.
If it be found so, some will dear abide it. [19]

SECOND PLEBEIAN.
Poor soul, his eyes are red as fire with weeping.

---

19. dear abide it. pay dearly for it

THIRD PLEBEIAN.
There's not a nobler man in Rome than Antony.

FOURTH PLEBEIAN.
Now mark him. He begins again to speak.

ANTONY.
But yesterday the word of Caesar might
Have stood against the world. Now lies he there,
And none so poor to do him reverence. [20]
O masters! If I were disposed to stir
Your hearts and minds to mutiny and rage, [21]
I should do Brutus wrong, and Cassius wrong,
Who, you all know, are honorable men.
I will not do them wrong; I rather choose
To wrong the dead, to wrong myself and you,
Than I will wrong such honorable men.
But here's a parchment with the seal of Caesar.
I found it in his closet; 'tis his will. [22]

[He shows the will]

Let but the commons hear this testament — [23]
Which, pardon me, I do not mean to read —
And they would go and kiss dead Caesar's wounds
And dip their napkins in his sacred blood, [24]
Yea, beg a hair of him for memory,
And dying, mention it within their wills,
Bequeathing it as a rich legacy
Unto their issue.

---

20. **none ... reverence.** no one, not even the lowliest person, is below Caesar now
21. **mutiny.** riot
22. **closet.** private chamber
23. **commons.** commoners
24. **napkins.** handkerchiefs

FOURTH PLEBEIAN.
We'll hear the will! Read it, Mark Antony.

ALL.
The will, the will! We will hear Caesar's will.

ANTONY.
Have patience, gentle friends; I must not read it.
It is not meet you know how Caesar loved you. [25]
You are not wood, you are not stones, but men;
And being men, hearing the will of Caesar,
It will inflame you, it will make you mad.
'Tis good you know not that you are his heirs,
For if you should, O, what would come of it?

FOURTH PLEBEIAN.
Read the will! We'll hear it, Antony.
You shall read us the will, Caesar's will.

ANTONY.
Will you be patient? Will you stay awhile?
I have o'ershot myself to tell you of it. [26]
I fear I wrong the honorable men
Whose daggers have stabbed Caesar; I do fear it.

FOURTH PLEBEIAN.
They were traitors. "Honorable men"!

ALL.
The will! The testament!

---

25. meet. fitting that
26. o'ershot myself. gone too far

SECOND PLEBEIAN.
They were villains, murderers. The will! Read the
will!

ANTONY.
You will compel me then to read the will?
Then make a ring about the corpse of Caesar
And let me show you him that made the will.
Shall I descend? And will you give me leave?

ALL.
Come down.

SECOND PLEBEIAN.
Descend.

THIRD PLEBEIAN.
You shall have leave.

[ANTONY *comes down. They gather around*
CAESAR]

FOURTH PLEBEIAN.
A ring; stand round.

FIRST PLEBEIAN.
Stand from the hearse. Stand from the body. [27]

SECOND PLEBEIAN.
Room for Antony, most noble Antony!

ANTONY.
Nay, press not so upon me. Stand far off. [28]

---

27. hearse. platform for a coffin
28. far. farther

ALL.

Stand back! Room! Bear back!

ANTONY.

If you have tears, prepare to shed them now.
You all do know this mantle. I remember [29]
The first time ever Caesar put it on;
'Twas on a summer's evening in his tent,
That day he overcame the Nervii. [30]
Look, in this place ran Cassius' dagger through.
See what a rent the envious Casca made. [31]
Through this the well-belovèd Brutus stabbed,
And as he plucked his cursèd steel away,
Mark how the blood of Caesar followed it,
As rushing out of doors to be resolved [32]
If Brutus so unkindly knocked or no; [33]
For Brutus, as you know, was Caesar's angel. [34]
Judge, O you gods, how dearly Caesar loved him!
This was the most unkindest cut of all; [35]
For when the noble Caesar saw him stab,
Ingratitude, more strong than traitor's arms,
Quite vanquished him. Then burst his mighty
    heart,
And in his mantle muffling up his face,
Even at the base of Pompey's statue,
Which all the while ran blood, great Caesar fell.

---

29. **mantle.** cloak, toga
30. **the Nervii.** the Belgian tribe which Caesar defeated in
    57 B.C.
31. **rent.** torn spot. **envious.** spiteful
32. **be resolved.** learn for certain
33. **unkindly.** cruelly and unnaturally
34. **angel.** other self
35. **unkindest.** cruel, unnatural

O, what a fall was there, my countrymen!
Then I, and you, and all of us fell down,
Whilst bloody treason flourished over us. [36]
O, now you weep, and I perceive you feel
The dint of pity. These are gracious drops. [37]
Kind souls, what weep you when you but behold [38]
Our Caesar's vesture wounded? Look you here, [39]
Here is himself, marred as you see with traitors.

[*He lifts* CAESAR'S *mantle*]

FIRST PLEBEIAN.
O piteous spectacle!

SECOND PLEBEIAN.
O noble Caesar!

THIRD PLEBEIAN.
O woeful day!

FOURTH PLEBEIAN.
O traitors, villains!

FIRST PLEBEIAN.
O most bloody sight!

SECOND PLEBEIAN.
We will be revenged.

ALL.
Revenge! About! [40] Seek! Burn! Fire! Kill! Slay!
Let not a traitor live!

---

36. flourished. triumphed, grew
37. dint. force
38. what. why
39. vesture. clothing
40. About. Let's go!

ANTONY.
Stay, countrymen.

FIRST PLEBEIAN.
Peace there! Hear the noble Antony.

SECOND PLEBEIAN.
We'll hear him, we'll follow him, we'll die with him!

ANTONY.
Good friends, sweet friends, let me not stir you up
To such a sudden flood of mutiny.
They that have done this deed are honorable.
What private griefs they have, alas, I know not, [41]
That made them do it. They are wise and honorable,
And will no doubt with reasons answer you.
I come not, friends, to steal away your hearts.
I am no orator, as Brutus is,
But, as you know me all, a plain blunt man
That love my friend, and that they know full well
That gave me public leave to speak of him. [42]
For I have neither wit, nor words, nor worth, [43]
Action, nor utterance, nor the power of speech [44]
To stir men's blood. I only speak right on.
I tell you that which you yourselves do know,
Show you sweet Caesar's wounds, poor poor dumb
   mouths,

---

41. griefs. grievances
42. public ... speak. permission to speak publicly
43. worth. high personal standing or reputation
44. Action, nor utterance. gestures nor vocal delivery of a
   skilled orator

And bid them speak for me. But were I Brutus,
And Brutus Antony, there were an Antony
Would ruffle up your spirits and put a tongue ⁴⁵
In every wound of Caesar that should move
The stones of Rome to rise and mutiny.

ALL.
We'll mutiny!

FIRST PLEBEIAN.
We'll burn the house of Brutus!

THIRD PLEBEIAN.
Away, then! Come, seek the conspirators.

ANTONY.
Yet hear me, countrymen. Yet hear me speak.

ALL.
Peace, ho! Hear Antony, most noble Antony!

ANTONY.
Why, friends, you go to do you know not what.
Wherein hath Caesar thus deserved your loves?
Alas, you know not. I must tell you then:
You have forgot the will I told you of.

ALL.
Most true, the will! Let's stay and hear the will.

ANTONY.
Here is the will, and under Caesar's seal.

---

45. **ruffle up.** stir to anger

To every Roman citizen he gives,
To every several man, seventy-five drachmas. [46]

SECOND PLEBEIAN.
Most noble Caesar! We'll revenge his death.

THIRD PLEBEIAN.
O royal Caesar!

ANTONY.
Hear me with patience.

ALL.
Peace, ho!

ANTONY.
Moreover, he hath left you all his walks,
His private arbors, and new-planted orchards, [47]
On this side Tiber; he hath left them you,
And to your heirs forever — common pleasures, [48]
To walk abroad and recreate yourselves.
Here was a Caesar! When comes such another?

FIRST PLEBEIAN.
Never, never! Come, away, away!
We'll burn his body in the holy place
And with the brands fire the traitors' houses.
Take up the body.

---

46. several. individual.   **drachmas.** Greek silver coins
   valued at about nineteen cents each in Shakespeare's
   time. This would have been a substantial amount of
   money in Elizabethan times.
47. orchards. gardens
48. common pleasures. public places of recreation

SECOND PLEBEIAN.
Go fetch fire!

THIRD PLEBEIAN.
Pluck down benches!

FOURTH PLEBEIAN.
Pluck down forms, windows, anything! [49]

> [*Exit* PLEBEIANS *with the body*]

ANTONY.
Now let it work. Mischief, thou art afoot.
Take thou what course thou wilt.

[*Enter* SERVANT]

> How now, fellow?

SERVANT.
Sir, Octavius is already come to Rome.

ANTONY.
Where is he?

SERVANT.
He and Lepidus are at Caesar's house.

ANTONY.
And thither will I straight to visit him. [50]
He comes upon a wish. Fortune is merry, [51]
And in this mood will give us anything.

---

49. forms. benches. **windows.** shutters
50. straight. go right away
51. upon a wish. just when wanted. **merry.** in a
favorable mood

SERVANT.
I heard him say Brutus and Cassius
Are rid like madmen through the gates of Rome. [52]

ANTONY.
Belike they had some notice of the people, [53]
How I had moved them. Bring me to Octavius.

[Exit]

---

52. **Are rid.** have ridden
53. **Belike.** probably.   **notice ... people.** word about the
    mood of the people

---◆---

Synopsis of Act III, Scene 2

The last scene showed how the people reacted to Caesar's death. At first, the crowds were sympathetic to Brutus. They shouted out that, in return for his "noble deed," they would create statues of him and "bring him to his house with shouts and clamours." Antony's speech began in a calm and sincere tone. The people became increasingly bitter as he mentioned all the good things Caesar had done for them. The tone turned to rage as Antony read Caesar's will. Meanwhile, Cassius and Brutus fled for their lives.

---◆---

———————◆———————

Before You Read Act III, Scene 3

This short scene shows the important part the mob plays in influencing the action of the play. Cinna, a poet and friend of Caesar's, is headed for the funeral. The mob approaches him and asks him questions. Note the questions they ask. "I am Cinna the poet! I am Cinna the poet!" he cries out. The mob has obviously confused Cinna with someone who has the same name. Who do they think he is? What does the mob do to Cinna?

———————◆———————

ACT III. Scene 3.

Location: A street.

[*Enter* CINNA *the poet, and after him the* PLEBEIANS]

CINNA.
I dreamt tonight that I did feast with Caesar, [1]
And things unluckily charge my fantasy. [2]
I have no will to wander forth of doors,
Yet something leads me forth.

FIRST PLEBEIAN.
What is your name?

SECOND PLEBEIAN.
Whither are you going?

THIRD PLEBEIAN.
Where do you dwell?

FOURTH PLEBEIAN.
Are you a married man or a bachelor?

SECOND PLEBEIAN.
Answer every man directly.

FIRST PLEBEIAN.
Ay, and briefly.

---

1. **tonight.** last night
2. **And things ... fantasy.** The events that have taken place weigh heavily on my imagination.

FOURTH PLEBEIAN.
Ay, and wisely.

THIRD PLEBEIAN.
Ay, and truly, you were best. [3]

CINNA.
What is my name? Whither am I going? Where do I dwell? Am I a married man or a bachelor? Then to answer every man directly and briefly, wisely and truly: wisely I say, I am a bachelor.

SECOND PLEBEIAN.
That's as much as to say they are fools that marry. You'll bear me a bang [4] for that, I fear. Proceed directly.

CINNA.
Directly, I am going to Caesar's funeral.

FIRST PLEBEIAN.
As a friend or any enemy?

CINNA.
As a friend.

SECOND PLEBEIAN.
That matter is answered directly.

FOURTH PLEBEIAN.
For your dwelling — briefly.

---

3. **you were best.** it would be best for you
4. **bear ... bang.** get a beating from me

CINNA.
Briefly, I dwell by the Capitol.

THIRD PLEBEIAN.
Your name, sir, truly.

CINNA.
Truly, my name is Cinna.

FIRST PLEBEIAN.
Tear him to pieces! He's a conspirator!

CINNA.
I am Cinna the poet, I am Cinna the poet!

FOURTH PLEBEIAN.
Tear him for his bad verses, tear him for his bad
verses!

CINNA.
I am not Cinna the conspirator.

FOURTH PLEBEIAN.
It is no matter, his name's Cinna. Pluck but his
name out of his heart, and turn him going. [5]

THIRD PLEBEIAN.
Tear him, tear him! Come, brands, ho, firebrands!
To Brutus', to Cassius'; burn all! Some to Decius'
house, and some to Casca's; some to Ligarius'.
Away, go!

[*Exit all the* PLEBEIANS, *dragging off* CINNA]

---

5. **turn him going.** send him on his way

————————◆————————

Synopsis of Act III, Scene 3

The previous scene provided a break in the action and separated the events of Caesar's murder from the rest of the play. In this scene, the mob attacked Cinna, a poet and friend of Caesar's, because they confused him with Cinna, the conspirator. The scene closed as the mob rushed to burn down the assassins' homes.

————————◆————————

Before You Read Act IV, Scene 1

Antony has joined forces with Octavius, Caesar's nephew, and Lepidus, a great general, and together they now rule Rome. (Historically, this event did not take place for a year after Caesar's death.) As the scene opens, these leaders, or triumvirs, are in Antony's house in Rome. They are preparing a list of names of people whom they want exiled or condemned to death. Many names are suggested. Notice which relatives Antony and Lepidus add to the list. This tells you about the moral character of these leaders. Note the reason why Antony sends Lepidus to Caesar's house to get his will. When Lepidus leaves, Antony says that he will not share power with Lepidus. Notice what Antony calls Lepidus and the type of job Antony thinks Lepidus is qualified for. Octavius reminds Antony that he thought enough of Lepidus to accept his suggestions for the list of condemned people, but Antony quickly adds that Lepidus would only be a burden to them. What praise does Octavius give in defense of Lepidus? How does Antony turn Octavius's praise into criticism? Note what Antony says that shows he has taken charge of the leadership. As this brief scene closes, Octavius warns that danger is near. What could this danger be?

ACT IV. Scene 1.

Location: A house in Rome.

[*Enter* ANTONY *with a list,* OCTAVIUS, *and* LEPIDUS]

ANTONY.
These many, then, shall die. Their names are
    pricked. [1]

OCTAVIUS.
Your brother too must die. Consent you, Lepidus?

LEPIDUS.
I do consent —

OCTAVIUS.
                    Prick him down, Antony.

LEPIDUS.
Upon condition Publius shall not live,
Who is your sister's son, Mark Antony.

ANTONY.
He shall not live. Look, with a spot I damn him. [2]
But Lepidus, go you to Caesar's house.
Fetch the will hither, and we shall determine [3]
How to cut off some charge in legacies.

LEPIDUS.
What, shall I find you here?

---

1. **pricked.** marked down on a list
2. **spot.** mark (on the list). **damn.** condemn
3. **determine ... legacies.** find a way to reduce the outlay
   of Caesar's estate, by altering the will

OCTAVIUS.
Or here or at the Capitol. [4]

[*Exit* LEPIDUS]

ANTONY.
This is a slight unmeritable man, [5]
Meet to be sent on errands. Is it fit,
The threefold world divided, he should stand [6]
One of the three to share it?

OCTAVIUS.
So you thought him,
And took his voice who should be pricked to die [7]
In our black sentence and proscription. [8]

ANTONY.
Octavius, I have seen more days than you; [9]
And though we lay these honors on this man
To ease ourselves of divers slanderous loads, [10]
He shall but bear them as the ass bears gold,
To groan and sweat under the business,
Either led or driven as we point the way;
And having brought our treasure where we will,

---

4. **Or.** either
5. **slight unmeritable.** insignificant and without merit
6. **The threefold world.** Europe, Asia and Africa (The
   triumvirs had divided up among themselves the lands on
   these three continents that had been conquered by
   Rome.)
7. **took his voice.** allowed him to vote or give his opinion
   about
8. **proscription.** list of those sentenced to death or exile
9. **have ... days.** am older than you
10. **divers ... loads.** various burdens of blame

Then take we down his load, and turn him off,
Like to the empty ass, to shake his ears
And graze in commons. [11]

OCTAVIUS.

You may do your will;
But he's a tried and valiant soldier.

ANTONY.

So is my horse, Octavius, and for that
I do appoint him store of provender. [12]
It is a creature that I teach to fight,
To wind, to stop, to run directly on, [13]
His corporal motion governed by my spirit. [14]
And in some taste is Lepidus but so. [15]
He must be taught, and trained, and bid go forth —
A barren-spirited fellow, one that feeds [16]
On objects, arts, and imitations,
Which, out of use and staled by other men, [17]
Begin his fashion. Do not talk of him [18]
But as a property. And now, Octavius, [19]
Listen great things. Brutus and Cassius [20]

---

11. **in commons.** on public pasture
12. **appoint ... provender.** allot him a supply of food
13. **wind.** turn
14. **corporal ... spirit.** movements governed by my mind
15. **taste.** degree
16. **barren-spirited ... imitations.** a person without ideas of his own who enjoys curiosities, arts, and styles
17. **out of use and staled.** made cheap or unworthy
18. **Begin his fashion.** He begins to use them (suggesting that he is hopelessly behind the times).
19. **property.** tool
20. **Listen.** hear

Are levying powers. We must straight make head. [21]
Therefore let our alliance be combined, [22]
Our best friends made, our means stretched; [23]
And let us presently go sit in council [24]
How covert matters may be best disclosed [25]
And open perils surest answerèd. [26]

OCTAVIUS.
Let us do so, for we are at the stake [27]
And bayed about with many enemies; [28]
And some that smile have in their hearts, I fear,
Millions of mischiefs. [29]

[*Exit*]

---

21. **levying powers.** enlisting troops. **straight make
    head.** quickly gather soldiers
22. **let ... combined.** let us work as one
23. **made.** brought together. **stretched.** used to fullest
    advantage
24. **presently.** at once
25. **How ... disclosed.** how secrets may be discovered
26. **perils surest answerèd.** dangers met
27. **at the stake.** like a bear tied to a stake
28. **bayed about.** surrounded by many dogs
29. **mischiefs.** plans to injure us

Synopsis of Act IV, Scene 1

The previous scene introduced the character of
Octavius Caesar into the plot. It also showed that
the new leaders, Mark Antony, Octavius Caesar,
and Lepidus, did not get along with each other. As
the scene opened, they were making a list of people
to be condemned. This revealed their very practical
approach to dealing with any opposition. They
included Antony's nephew and Lepidus's brother
on the list. Lepidus was sent to get Caesar's will so
that they could stop some of Caesar's money from
going to the people. After he left, Antony said that
Lepidus was not of much use to them, but Octavius
disagreed with him. Antony then ordered that they
meet in council to discuss a strategy for attacking
Brutus's and Cassius's armies.

---◆---

Before You Read Act IV, Scene 2

It is several months later at a military camp near Sardis. Brutus and Cassius have been traveling separately with their armies and have not seen each other for a long time. Lucilius, Brutus's officer, and Pindarus, Cassius's servant, stand before Brutus. Lucilius has just returned from a visit to Cassius's army. Brutus greets the men and says that he suspects Cassius's feelings toward him have changed. Notice Pindarus's response. Brutus explains his feelings. Note what happens, according to Brutus, when friendships change.

Cassius approaches Brutus's camp with his cavalry and Brutus's officers march to meet him. Without a greeting, Cassius abruptly says to Brutus, "You have done me wrong." How does Brutus respond to this accusation?

---◆---

ACT IV. Scene 2.

Location: Camp near Sardis. In front of Brutus's tent.

[*Drum. Enter* BRUTUS, LUCILIUS, LUCIUS, *and the army.* TITINIUS *and* PINDARUS *meet them*]

BRUTUS.
    Stand, ho! [1]

LUCILIUS.
                Give the word, ho, and stand!

BRUTUS.
    What now, Lucilius, is Cassius near?

LUCILIUS.
    He is at hand, and Pindarus is come
    To do you salutation from his master.

BRUTUS.
    He greets me well. Your master, Pindarus, [2]
    In his own change, or by ill officers, [3]
    Hath given me some worthy cause to wish
    Things done, undone; but if he be at hand
    I shall be satisfied. [4]

---

1. **Stand ... stand.** halt! Pass the word
2. **well.** formally, through Pindarus
3. **In his own ... done, undone.** has changed in his feelings toward me, or has received bad advice from subordinates and has made me wish we had not done what we did
4. **be satisfied.** have things explained to my satisfaction

PINDARUS.
                    I do not doubt
But that my noble master will appear
Such as he is, full of regard and honor. ⁵

BRUTUS.
He is not doubted. —A word, Lucilius.

                    [BRUTUS *and* LUCILIUS *speak apart*]

How he received you let me be resolved. ⁶

LUCILIUS.
With courtesy and with respect enough,
But not with such familiar instances ⁷
Nor with such free and friendly conference ⁸
As he hath used of old.

BRUTUS.
                    Thou hast described
A hot friend cooling. Ever note, Lucilius,
When love begins to sicken and decay
It useth an enforcèd ceremony. ⁹
There are no tricks in plain and simple faith.
But hollow men, like horses hot at hand, ¹⁰
Make gallant show and promise of their mettle;
                    [*Low march within*]

But when they should endure the bloody spur,

---

5. **regard.** consideration
6. **resolved.** fully informed
7. **familiar instances.** marks of friendship
8. **conference.** conversation
9. **enforcèd ceremony.** forced formality
10. **hollow.** insincere.   **hot at hand.** full of spirit when held in

They fall their crests and like deceitful jades [11]
Sink in the trial. Comes his army on? [12]

LUCILIUS.
They mean this night in Sardis to be quartered. [13]
The greater part, the horse in general, [14]
Are come with Cassius.

[*Enter* CASSIUS *and his powers*]

BRUTUS.
                      Hark, he is arrived.
March gently on to meet him. [15]

CASSIUS.
Stand, ho!

BRUTUS.
Stand, ho! Speak the word along.

FIRST SOLDIER.
Stand!

SECOND SOLDIER.
Stand!

THIRD SOLDIER.
Stand!

CASSIUS.
Most noble brother, you have done me wrong.

---

11. **fall their crests.** hang their heads.   **jades.** worthless horses
12. **Sink.** give way
13. **Sardis.** the capital city of Lydia in Asia Minor
14. **the horse in general.** the cavalry
15. **gently.** slowly, without hostility

BRUTUS.
Judge me, you gods! Wrong I mine enemies?
And if not so, how should I wrong a brother?

CASSIUS.
Brutus, this sober form of yours hides wrongs; [16]
And when you do them —

BRUTUS.
                    Cassius, be content.
Speak your griefs softly. I do know you well. [17]
Before the eyes of both our armies here,
(Which should perceive nothing but love from us,)
Let us not wrangle. Bid them move away.
Then in my tent, Cassius, enlarge your griefs, [18]
And I will give you audience.

CASSIUS.
                    Pindarus,
Bid our commanders lead their charges off [19]
A little from this ground.

BRUTUS.
Lucius, do you the like, and let no man
Come to our tent till we have done our conference.
Let Lucilius and Titinius guard our door.

[*Exit.* BRUTUS *and* CASSIUS *remain.* LUCILIUS
and TITINIUS *stand guard at the door*]

---

16. **sober form.** serious manner
17. **griefs.** complaints
18. **enlarge.** freely express
19. **charges.** troops

———————◆———————

Synopsis of Act IV, Scene 2

The previous scene showed that bad feelings were drawing the conspirators apart. Lucilius, Brutus's officer, had just returned from Cassius's camp along with Cassius's servant, Pindarus. Brutus asked Lucilius how Cassius had treated him, suspecting that their friendship had somehow changed. Lucilius said that Cassius treated him with courtesy but not with friendship. Brutus then spoke about failing friendships. Cassius arrived with his troops and, without greeting Brutus first, accused him of some wrongdoing. They went inside Brutus's tent so that the troops would not see them quarreling.

———————◆———————

---◆---

Before You Read Act IV, Scene 3

This lengthy quarrel scene is possibly one of the most famous scenes in all of Shakespeare's plays. It shows two loyal friends, once committed to a noble purpose, now caught up in petty bickering. Cassius is angry that Brutus had publicly criticized one of his friends, Lucius Pella, for taking a bribe. Cassius says that every small fault does not need to be criticized in public. Then Brutus accuses Cassius of some wrongdoing. Notice the parallels Brutus trys to draw between Cassius and Caesar. Brutus and Cassius continue to quarrel. Cassius warns, "I may do what you will be sorry for." But Brutus is not bothered by Cassius's threats.

Brutus reveals that he has done something out of character, but as a result of necessity. Pay attention to Brutus's words that tell what he did. Cassius denies that he did not comply with Brutus's request and his strong loyalties toward Brutus begin to surface. Notice Brutus's and Cassius's words that show how each feels about friendship. Pay attention to what Cassius does that causes the angry, defiant tone of the argument to lift.

Brutus tells Cassius about a great personal loss. Notice who has died and the reasons for that death. Pay attention to how differently Brutus and Cassius react to the news.

Titinius and Messala, officers and friends of

Brutus and Cassius, enter the tent to report that Octavius and Mark Antony are heading toward their camp but they are swinging down through Philippi. They bring horrifying news about Antony's and Octavius's vicious rampage. Notice the strategy Brutus suggests for meeting Antony's army. Think about why this plan might not be a good idea and why Cassius agrees to it.

Lucius enters with Brutus's nightclothes and the others leave, except for Claudius and Varro, the two sentries, whom Brutus asks to sleep on cushions in the tent. Lucius plays a tune and, as Brutus begins to read, a strange visitor enters the tent. Note who this visitor is and the reason he has come. Why does Brutus wake the others?

———————◆———————

ACT IV. Scene 3.

Location: Inside Brutus's tent.

CASSIUS.
That you have wronged me doth appear in this:
You have condemned and noted Lucius Pella [1]
For taking bribes here of the Sardians,
Wherein my letters, praying on his side, [2]
Because I knew the man, were slighted off. [3]

BRUTUS.
You wronged yourself to write in such a case.

CASSIUS.
In such a time as this it is not meet [4]
That every nice offense should bear his comment. [5]

BRUTUS.
Let me tell you, Cassius, you yourself
Are much condemned to have an itching palm, [6]
To sell and mart your offices for gold [7]
To undeservers.

CASSIUS.
               I an itching palm?

---

1. **noted.** publicly criticized. **Lucius Pella.** a Roman praetor in Sardis
2. **letters ... side.** letter pleading on his behalf
3. **slighted off.** disregarded
4. **meet.** fitting
5. **nice offense.** petty fault. **bear his comment.** receive its criticism
6. **condemned ... palm.** accused of accepting bribes
7. **mart.** trade

You know that you are Brutus that speaks this,
Or, by the gods, this speech were else your last. [8]

BRUTUS.
The name of Cassius honors this corruption, [9]
And chastisement doth therefore hide his head. [10]

CASSIUS.
Chastisement!

BRUTUS.
Remember March, the ides of March remember.
Did not great Julius bleed for justice' sake?
What villain touched his body that did stab
And not for justice? What, shall one of us,
That struck the foremost man of all this world
But for supporting robbers, shall we now [11]
Contaminate our fingers with base bribes,
And sell the mighty space of our large honors [12]
For so much trash as may be graspèd thus? [13]
I had rather be a dog and bay the moon [14]
Than such a Roman.

---

8. **else.** otherwise
9. **honors.** gives respectability to
10. **chastisement ... head.** Officials dare not punish lesser
    men who commit these crimes.
11. **But.** only. **robbers.** Brutus suggests that Caesar's
    officials were also involved in taking bribes and that this
    was a motive in his assassination.
12. **the mighty ... honors.** the greatness of our offices
13. **trash.** illegal money
14. **bay.** howl at

CASSIUS.

Brutus, bait not me. [15]

I'll not endure it. You forget yourself
To hedge me in. I am a soldier, I, [16]
Older in practice, abler than yourself
To make conditions. [17]

BRUTUS.

Go to! You are not, Cassius.

CASSIUS.
I am.

BRUTUS.
I say you are not.

CASSIUS.
Urge me no more; I shall forget myself. [18]
Have mind upon your health. Tempt me no
farther. [19]

BRUTUS.
Away, slight man! [20]

CASSIUS.
Is 't possible?

---

15. **bait.** provoke (as a bear tied to a stake is harassed by a
dog)
16. **hedge me in.** limit my actions
17. **conditions.** decisions (about the behavior of men such
as Lucius Pella, for example)
18. **Urge.** annoy
19. **Tempt.** provoke
20. **slight.** insignificant

BRUTUS.
Hear me, for I will speak.
Must I give way and room to your rash choler? [21]
Shall I be frighted when a madman stares? [22]

CASSIUS.
O ye gods, ye gods! Must I endure all this?

BRUTUS.
All this? Ay, more. Fret till your proud heart break.
Go show your slaves how choleric you are
And make your bondmen tremble. Must I budge? [23]
Must I observe you? Must I stand and crouch [24]
Under your testy humor? By the gods, [25]
You shall digest the venom of your spleen [26]
Though it do split you; for, from this day forth,
I'll use you for my mirth, yea, for my laughter,
When you are waspish. [27]

CASSIUS.
Is it come to this?

BRUTUS.
You say you are a better soldier.
Let it appear so; make your vaunting true, [28]

---

21. **give way and room to.** make allowance for and accept.
    choler. anger
22. **stares.** looks wildly at me
23. **budge.** flinch away
24. **observe.** pay reverence to. **crouch.** bow
25. **testy humor.** irritability
26. **digest.** eat. **spleen.** the poison of your own anger (The
    spleen was thought to be the source of anger.)
27. **waspish.** bad-tempered
28. **vaunting.** boasting

And it shall please me well. For mine own part,
I shall be glad to learn of noble men. [29]

CASSIUS.
You wrong me every way! You wrong me, Brutus.
I said an elder soldier, not a better.
Did I say "better"?

BRUTUS.
                    If you did, I care not.

CASSIUS.
When Caesar lived he durst not thus have moved me. [30]

BRUTUS.
Peace, peace! You durst not so have tempted him. [31]

CASSIUS.
I durst not?

BRUTUS.
No.

CASSIUS.
What, durst not tempt him?

BRUTUS.
                    For your life you durst not.

CASSIUS.
Do not presume too much upon my love.
I may do that I shall be sorry for.

---

29. learn of. hear about (those who have proved themselves
    noble)
30. moved. annoyed
31. tempted. provoked

BRUTUS.
You have done that you should be sorry for.
There is no terror, Cassius, in your threats,
For I am armed so strong in honesty
That they pass by me as the idle wind,
Which I respect not. I did send to you [32]
For certain sums of gold, which you denied me;
For I can raise no money by vile means.
By heaven, I had rather coin my heart
And drop my blood for drachmas than to wring
From the hard hands of peasants their vile trash
By any indirection. I did send [33]
To you for gold to pay my legions,
Which you denied me. Was that done like Cassius?
Should I have answered Caius Cassius so?
When Marcus Brutus grows so covetous
To lock such rascal counters from his friends, [34]
Be ready, gods, with all your thunderbolts;
Dash him to pieces!

CASSIUS.
                    I denied you not.

BRUTUS.
You did.

CASSIUS.
          I did not. He was but a fool
That brought my answer back. Brutus hath rived
    my heart. [35]

---

32. respect not. disregard
33. indirection. irregular means
34. rascal counters. worthless coins
35. rived. broken

A friend should bear his friend's infirmities,
But Brutus makes mine greater than they are.

BRUTUS.
I do not, till you practice them on me.

CASSIUS.
You love me not.

BRUTUS.
     I do not like your faults.

CASSIUS.
A friendly eye could never see such faults.

BRUTUS.
A flatterer's would not, though they do appear
As huge as high Olympus.

CASSIUS.
Come, Antony, and young Octavius, come,
Revenge yourselves alone on Cassius,
For Cassius is aweary of the world:
Hated by one he loves, braved by his brother, [36]
Checked like a bondman, all his faults observed, [37]
Set in a notebook, learned and conned by rote [38]
To cast into my teeth. O, I could weep
My spirit from mine eyes! There is my dagger,

   [*He offers his unsheathed dagger*]

---

36. braved. bullied
37. Checked like a bondman. scolded like a slave
38. conned by rote. memorized

And here my naked breast; within, a heart
Dearer than Pluto's mine, richer than gold. [39]
If that thou be'st a Roman, take it forth.
I, that denied thee gold, will give my heart. [40]
Strike, as thou didst at Caesar; for I know,
When thou didst hate him worst, thou lovedst him
    better
Than ever thou lovedst Cassius.

BRUTUS.

Sheathe your dagger.
Be angry when you will, it shall have scope. [41]
Do what you will, dishonor shall be humor. [42]
O Cassius, you are yokèd with a lamb [43]
That carries anger as the flint bears fire,
Who, much enforcèd, shows a hasty spark [44]
And straight is cold again. [45]

CASSIUS.

Hath Cassius lived
To be but mirth and laughter to his Brutus
When grief and blood ill-tempered vexeth him? [46]

---

39. Dearer. wealthier.   **Pluto.** god of the underworld
40. that denied. who you claim denied
41. scope. free play
42. dishonor ... humor. any dishonorable acts I'll regard as
    your irritable disposition
43. yokèd with. in partnership with
44. enforcèd. provoked
45. straight. at once
46. blood ill-tempered. uneven disposition due to an
    imbalance inside the body

BRUTUS.
When I spoke that, I was ill-tempered too.

CASSIUS.
Do you confess so much? Give me your hand.

BRUTUS.
And my heart too.

CASSIUS.
     O Brutus!

BRUTUS.
       What's the matter?

CASSIUS.
Have not you love enough to bear with me,
When that rash humor which my mother gave me [47]
Makes me forgetful?

BRUTUS.
      Yes, Cassius, and from
 henceforth,
When you are overearnest with your Brutus,
He'll think your mother chides, and leave you so. [48]

[*Enter a* POET, *followed by* LUCILIUS *and*
TITINIUS, *who have been standing guard at the door*]

POET.
Let me go in to see the generals!
There is some grudge between 'em; 'tis not meet
They be alone.

---

47. rash humor. anger
48. your mother ... so. it is just your inherited disposition,
 and let it go at that

LUCILIUS.
> You shall not come to them.

POET.
> Nothing but death shall stay me.

CASSIUS.
> How now? What's the matter?

POET.
> For shame, you generals! What do you mean?
> Love and be friends, as two such men should be;
> For I have seen more years, I'm sure, than ye.

CASSIUS.
> Ha, ha, how vilely doth this cynic rhyme! [49]

BRUTUS.
> Get you hence, sirrah. Saucy fellow, hence!

CASSIUS.
> Bear with him, Brutus. 'Tis his fashion.

BRUTUS.
> I'll know his humor when he knows his time. [50]
> What should the wars do with these jigging fools? [51]
> Companion, hence! [52]

CASSIUS.
> Away, away, begone!

---

49. cynic. rude fellow (one outspoken against luxury)
50. I'll ... time. I'll accept his eccentric behavior when he
   chooses the appropriate time to display it.
51. jigging. rhyming
52. Companion. fellow (spoken with contempt)

[*Exit* POET]

BRUTUS.
Lucilius and Titinius, bid the commanders
Prepare to lodge their companies tonight.

CASSIUS.
And come yourselves, and bring Messala with you
Immediately to us.

[*Exit* LUCILIUS *and* TITINIUS]

BRUTUS.
[*To* LUCIUS *within*] Lucius, a bowl of wine.

CASSIUS.
I did not think you could have been so angry.

BRUTUS.
O Cassius, I am sick of many griefs.

CASSIUS.
Of your philosophy you make no use
If you give place to accidental evils. [53]

BRUTUS.
No man bears sorrow better. Portia is dead.

CASSIUS.
Ha? Portia?

BRUTUS.
She is dead.

---

53. Of your philosophy ... accidental evils. Brutus's
philosophy was Stoicism. As a Stoic he believed that
nothing evil would happen to a good man.

CASSIUS.
How scaped I killing when I crossed you so? [54]
O insupportable and touching loss! [55]
Upon what sickness?

BRUTUS.
Impatient of my absence, [56]
And grief that young Octavius with Mark Antony
Have made themselves so strong—for with her
death [57]
That tidings came—with this she fell distract
And, her attendants absent, swallowed fire. [58]

CASSIUS.
And died so?

BRUTUS.
Even so.

CASSIUS.
O ye immortal gods!

[*Enter* LUCIUS *with wine and tapers*]

BRUTUS.
Speak no more of her. —Give me a bowl of wine. —
In this I bury all unkindness, Cassius.

[*Drinks*]

---

54. **How scaped ... you so.** How did I escape being killed
    when I opposed you?
55. **touching.** severe
56. **Impatient of.** unable to endure
57. **her death.** news of her death
58. **swallowed fire.** put hot coals in her mouth and choked
    to death

CASSIUS.
My heart is thirsty for that noble pledge.
Fill, Lucius, till the wine o'erswell the cup;
I cannot drink too much of Brutus' love.

[*He drinks. Exit* LUCIUS]

[*Enter* TITINIUS *and* MESSALA]

BRUTUS.
Come in, Titinius. Welcome, good Messala.
Now sit we close about this taper here
And call in question our necessities. ⁵⁹

[*They sit*]

CASSIUS.
Portia, art thou gone?

BRUTUS.
                    No more, I pray you.
Messala, I have here receivèd letters
That young Octavius and Mark Antony
Come down upon us with a mighty power, ⁶⁰
Bending their expedition toward Philippi. ⁶¹

[*He shows letters*]

MESSALA.
Myself have letters of the selfsame tenor.

BRUTUS.
With what addition?

---

59. call in question. examine
60. power. army
61. Bending. turning. **expedition.** troops

MESSALA.
That by proscription and bills of outlawry
Octavius, Antony, and Lepidus
Have put to death an hundred senators.

BRUTUS.
Therein our letters do not well agree;
Mine speak of seventy senators that died
By their proscriptions, Cicero being one.

CASSIUS.
Cicero one?

MESSALA.
                    Cicero is dead,
And by that order of proscription.
Had you your letters from your wife, my lord?

BRUTUS.
No, Messala.

MESSALA.
Nor nothing in your letters writ of her? [62]

BRUTUS.
Nothing, Messala.

MESSALA.
                    That, methinks, is strange.

BRUTUS.
Why ask you? Hear you aught of her in yours?

---

62. nothing ... her. nothing mentioned about her in the
letters you've received

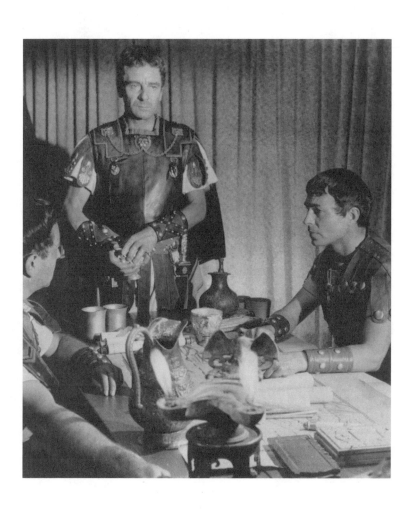

MESSALA.
No, my lord.

BRUTUS.
Now, as you are a Roman, tell me true.

MESSALA.
Then like a Roman bear the truth I tell,
For certain she is dead, and by strange manner.

BRUTUS.
Why, farewell, Portia. We must die, Messala.
With meditating that she must die once, [63]
I have the patience to endure it now.

MESSALA.
Even so great men great losses should endure. [64]

CASSIUS.
I have as much of this in art as you, [65]
But yet my nature could not bear it so.

BRUTUS.
Well, to our work alive. What do you think [66]
Of marching to Philippi presently?

---

63. once. eventually
64. Even so. in just such a way
65. have ... art. have as much Stoicism in theory (As a Stoic, Brutus believed that everything is controlled by natural laws and the wise man should follow a virtuous path through a life governed by reasoning and by remaining indifferent to emotions.)
66. to our work alive. Let us go about the work we must do as living men.

CASSIUS.
I do not think it good.

BRUTUS.
                    Your reason?

CASSIUS.
                    This it is:
'Tis better that the enemy seek us.
So shall he waste his means, weary his soldiers,
Doing himself offense, whilst we, lying still, [67]
Are full of rest, defense, and nimbleness.

BRUTUS.
Good reasons must of force give place to better. [68]
The people twixt Philippi and this ground
Do stand but in a forced affection,
For they have grudged us contribution.
The enemy, marching along by them,
By them shall make a fuller number up,
Come on refreshed, new-added, and encouraged; [69]
From which advantage shall we cut him off
If at Philippi we do face him there,
These people at our back.

CASSIUS.
                    Hear me, good brother.

BRUTUS.
Under your pardon. You must note besides [70]
That we have tried the utmost of our friends;

---

67. offense. harm
68. of force. of necessity
69. new-added. reinforced
70. Under your pardon. excuse me

Our legions are brim full, our cause is ripe.
The enemy increaseth every day;
We, at the height, are ready to decline.
There is a tide in the affairs of men
Which, taken at the flood, leads on to fortune;
Omitted, all the voyage of their life [71]
Is bound in shallows and in miseries. [72]
On such a full sea are we now afloat,
And we must take the current when it serves
Or lose our ventures. [73]

CASSIUS.

Then, with your will, go on. [74]
We'll along ourselves and meet them at Philippi. [75]

BRUTUS.

The deep of night is crept upon our talk,
And nature must obey necessity,
Which we will niggard with a little rest. [76]
There is no more to say?

CASSIUS.

No more. Good night.
Early tomorrow will we rise and hence. [77]

BRUTUS.

Lucius! [Enter LUCIUS] My gown. [78]

---

71. **Omitted.** neglected
72. **bound in.** confined to
73. **our ventures.** what we have invested
74. **with your will.** as you wish
75. **along.** go along
76. **niggard ... rest.** satisfy stingily with a short sleep
77. **hence.** leave
78. **gown.** dressing gown

[Exit LUCIUS]
Farewell, good

Messala.
Good night, Titinius. Noble, noble Cassius,
Good night and good repose.

CASSIUS.

O my dear brother!
This was an ill beginning of the night.
Never come such division 'tween our souls!
Let it not, Brutus.

[*Enter* LUCIUS *with the gown*]

BRUTUS.

Everything is well.

CASSIUS.
Good night, my lord.

BRUTUS.

Good night, good

brother.

TITINIUS, MESSALA.
Good night, Lord Brutus.

BRUTUS.

Farewell, everyone.
[*Exit all but* BRUTUS *and* LUCIUS]

Give me the gown. Where is thy instrument? [79]

LUCIUS.
Here in the tent.

---

79. instrument. lute

BRUTUS.
>What, thou speak'st drowsily?
>Poor knave, I blame thee not; thou art o'erwatched. [80]
>Call Claudius and some other of my men;
>I'll have them sleep on cushions in my tent.

LUCIUS.
>Varro and Claudius!

[*Enter* VARRO *and* CLAUDIUS]

VARRO.
>Calls my lord?

BRUTUS.
>I pray you, sirs, lie in my tent and sleep.
>It may be I shall raise you by and by [81]
>On business to my brother Cassius.

VARRO.
>So please you, we will stand and watch your
>   pleasure. [82]

BRUTUS.
>I will not have it so. Lie down, good sirs.
>It may be I shall otherwise bethink me. [83]

>[VARRO *and* CLAUDIUS *lie down*]

>Look, Lucius, here's the book I sought for so;
>I put it in the pocket of my gown.

---

80. knave. servant.   **o'erwatched.** weary from too much
  watchfulness
81. raise. wake
82. watch your pleasure. wait for your orders
83. otherwise bethink me. change my mind

LUCIUS.
I was sure your lordship did not give it me.

BRUTUS.
Bear with me, good boy, I am much forgetful.
Canst thou hold up thy heavy eyes awhile
And touch thy instrument a strain or two? [84]

LUCIUS.
Ay, my lord, an 't please you. [85]

BRUTUS.
It does, my boy.
I trouble thee too much, but thou art willing.

LUCIUS.
It is my duty, sir.

BRUTUS.
I should not urge thy duty past thy might;
I know young bloods look for a time of rest. [86]

LUCIUS.
I have slept, my lord, already.

BRUTUS.
It was well done, and thou shalt sleep again;
I will not hold thee long. If I do live,
I will be good to thee.

[*Music, and a song.* LUCIUS *falls asleep*]

---

84. **touch.** play.   **strain.** tune
85. **an 't.** if it
86. **young bloods.** youthful constitutions

This is a sleepy tune. O murderous slumber, [87]
Layest thou thy leaden mace upon my boy, [88]
That plays thee music? Gentle knave, good night;
I will not do thee so much wrong to wake thee.
If thou dost nod, thou break'st thy instrument;
I'll take it from thee. And, good boy, good night.

> [*He removes* LUCIUS' *instrument,*
> *and begins to read*]

Let me see, let me see; is not the leaf turned down
Where I left reading? Here it is, I think.

[*Enter the* GHOST OF CAESAR]

How ill this taper burns! Ha! who comes here? [89]
I think it is the weakness of mine eyes
That shapes this monstrous apparition.
It comes upon me. — Art thou any thing? [90]
Art thou some god, some angel, or some devil,
That mak'st my blood cold and my hair to stare? [91]
Speak to me what thou art.

GHOST.
Thy evil spirit, Brutus.

---

87. **murderous slumber.** deathlike sleep
88. **leaden mace.** heavy staff of office (refers to the practice
    of tapping with a mace the shoulder of one being placed
    under arrest)
89. **How ... apparition.** Lights burning low and blue
    indicate the presence of a ghost.
90. **upon.** toward
91. **stare.** stand on end

BRUTUS.

Why com'st thou?

GHOST.

To tell thee thou shalt see me at Philippi.

BRUTUS.

Well; then I shall see thee again?

GHOST.

Ay, at Philippi.

BRUTUS.

Why, I will see thee at Philippi, then.

[*Exit* GHOST]

Now I have taken heart, thou vanishest.
Ill spirit, I would hold more talk with thee.
Boy, Lucius! Varro! Claudius! Sirs, awake!
Claudius!

LUCIUS.

The strings, my lord, are false. [92]

BRUTUS.

He thinks he still is at his instrument.
Lucius, awake!

LUCIUS.

My lord?

BRUTUS.

Didst thou dream, Lucius, that thou so criedst out?

---

92. false. out of tune

LUCIUS.
My lord, I do not know that I did cry.

BRUTUS.
Yes, that thou didst. Didst thou see anything?

LUCIUS.
Nothing, my lord.

BRUTUS.
Sleep again, Lucius. Sirrah Claudius!
[*To* VARRO] Fellow thou, awake!

VARRO.
My lord?

CLAUDIUS.
My lord?

[*They get up*]

BRUTUS.
Why did you so cry out, sirs, in your sleep?

VARRO, CLAUDIUS.
Did we, my lord?

BRUTUS.
Ay. Saw you anything?

VARRO.
No, my lord, I saw nothing.

CLAUDIUS.
Nor I, my lord.

BRUTUS.
Go and commend me to my brother Cassius. [93]
Bid him set on his powers betimes before, [94]
And we will follow.

VARRO, CLAUDIUS.
     It shall be done, my lord.
           [Exit]

---

93. commend me. deliver my greetings
94. set ... before. advance his troops

---◆---

Synopsis of Act IV, Scene 3

In the previous scene we looked into the inner lives of Brutus and Cassius. At first they argued, accusing each other of wrongdoing. Cassius accused Brutus of publicly condemning his friend for taking bribes and Brutus accused Cassius of taking money from the people using unjust methods. Cassius threatened Brutus, but Brutus remained unmoved. Cassius changed his tone because he thought Brutus had lost respect for him. Soon they made up their differences and their friendship was restored. After a meddling poet entered and tried to stop the generals from arguing, Brutus mentioned that Portia had died. Cassius was extremely upset by this news and could not understand Brutus's self control. Finally, their officers brought the news that the enemy army was advancing, and Brutus and Cassius began to plan their strategy. Cassius reluctantly agreed with Brutus's plan to meet the army at Philippi. Later, while Brutus was reading in his tent, the ghost of Caesar appeared. The ghost warned Brutus that he would meet him at Philippi.

---◆---

———————————◆———————————

Before You Read Act V, Scene 1

A tragedy is a play in which the main character is involved in a struggle of great importance that ends in disaster. This main character is usually a noble person whose downfall is the result of a tragic flaw, or weakness. This tragic flaw may be ambition, pride, or jealousy, which often result in numerous interweaving conflicts.

All of the conflicts in *The Tragedy of Julius Caesar* are resolved in Act V. Think about the conflicts as you answer the questions posed in the Introduction: Who is the tragic hero of the play? What is his character flaw? How does this weakness of character lead to his downfall?

Act V brings us to the battlefield on the plains of Philippi. Octavius and Antony wait with their armies for Brutus and Cassius to come down from the hills to attack. Antony claims that he knows exactly what the conspirators are planning to do. Notice what he says about their show of bravery and strength. Antony orders Octavius to lead his troops along the left of the battlefield. Octavius disagrees. How does Antony respond to Octavius's refusal to obey him? Is Octavius reminding Antony of his right to rule?

Drums sound announcing the arrival of Brutus and Cassius along with Lucilius, Titinius, Messala and the conspirators' army. A messenger warns that their red flag, the "bloody sign of battle is hung out." Brutus approaches Antony. (It was a common practice, in ancient wars, for leaders of opposing armies to insult each other before battle.) Pay special attention to what Antony says to Brutus that expresses the theme in the play of using words to deceive. Notice the words Cassius and Brutus use to describe Antony. How does Antony respond?

After the exchange of words with Brutus, Octavius and Antony leave to take their position. Brutus talks with Lucilius, his second in command, and Cassius speaks to Messala. Notice that Cassius has changed his beliefs about omens. What does he feel is a bad omen for his army now and foretells its death?

Brutus and Cassius talk of defeat and death, almost as if they have lost the will to fight. They put on a brave face and bid affectionate farewells. Do the conspirators sense that they will see each other again?

ACT V. Scene 1.

Location: The plains of Philippi.

[*Enter* OCTAVIUS, ANTONY, *and their army*]

OCTAVIUS.
Now, Antony, our hopes are answerèd.
You said the enemy would not come down,
But keep the hills and upper regions. [1]
It proves not so. Their battles are at hand; [2]
They mean to warn us at Philippi here,
Answering before we do demand of them. [3]

ANTONY.
Tut, I am in their bosoms, and I know [4]
Wherefore they do it. They could be content
To visit other places, and come down [5]
With fearful bravery, thinking by this face [6]
To fasten in our thoughts that they have courage; [7]
But 'tis not so. [8]

[*Enter a* MESSENGER]

---

1. **keep.** remain in
2. **battles.** armies
3. **They ... them.** They appear in opposition to us before we challenge them.
4. **I ... bosoms.** I know what they are thinking.
5. **visit other places.** be elsewhere. **come.** they come
6. **fearful bravery.** awesome show of bravery to hide their fear. **face.** appearance
7. **fasten ... thoughts.** convince us
8. **'tis not so.** their plan cannot deceive us, or they have no courage

MESSENGER.
Prepare you, generals.
The enemy comes on in gallant show.
Their bloody sign of battle is hung out, [9]
And something to be done immediately. [10]

ANTONY.
Octavius, lead your battle softly on [11]
Upon the left hand of the even field.

OCTAVIUS.
Upon the right hand, I. Keep thou the left.

ANTONY.
Why do you cross me in this exigent? [12]

OCTAVIUS.
I do not cross you, but I will do so. [13]   [*March*]

[*Drum. Enter* BRUTUS, CASSIUS, *and their
army;* LUCILIUS, TITINIUS, MESSALA, *and
others*]

BRUTUS.
They stand and would have parley.

CASSIUS.
Stand fast, Titinius. We must out and talk. [14]

---

9. **bloody sign.** A red flag was flown from the tent of a
   Roman general to signal the start of battle.
10. **to be.** is to be
11. **softly.** slowly
12. **cross.** contradict.   **exigent.** critical situation
13. **do so.** do as I said
14. **out.** go out

OCTAVIUS.
Mark Antony, shall we give sign of battle?

ANTONY.
No, Caesar, we will answer on their charge. [15]
Make forth. The generals would have some words. [16]

OCTAVIUS.
[*To his officers*] Stir not until the signal.

[*The two sides advance toward one another*]

BRUTUS.
Words before blows. Is it so, countrymen?

OCTAVIUS.
Not that we love words better, as you do.

BRUTUS.
Good words are better than bad strokes, Octavius.

ANTONY.
In your bad strokes, Brutus, you give good words.
Witness the hole you made in Caesar's heart,
Crying, "Long live! Hail, Caesar!"

CASSIUS.
                                    Antony,
The posture of your blows are yet unknown; [17]
But for your words, they rob the Hybla bees, [18]
And leave them honeyless.

---

15. **answer on their charge.** meet their advance
16. **Make forth.** go forward
17. **posture.** quality
18. **for.** as for. **Hybla bees.** Bees from this town in
    ancient Sicily are famous for their sweet honey.

ANTONY.

Not stingless too?

BRUTUS.

O, yes, and soundless too.
For you have stolen their buzzing, Antony,
And very wisely threat before you sting. [19]

ANTONY.

Villains! You did not so when your vile daggers [20]
Hacked one another in the sides of Caesar.
You showed your teeth like apes, and fawned like
    hounds, [21]
And bowed like bondmen, kissing Caesar's feet,
Whilst damnèd Casca, like a cur, behind
Struck Caesar on the neck. O you flatterers!

CASSIUS.

Flatterers? Now, Brutus, thank yourself!
This tongue had not offended so today
If Cassius might have ruled. [22]

OCTAVIUS.

Come, come, the cause. If arguing make us sweat, [23]
The proof of it will turn to redder drops. [24]
Look,

[He draws]

---

19. **very wisely.** said ironically; Brutus suggests that
    Antony is all talk and no action. **threat.** threaten
20. **so.** give warning
21. **showed your teeth.** grinned
22. **If ... ruled.** if Cassius had had his way when he urged
    that Antony be killed
23. **the cause.** business at hand
24. **proof.** test

I draw a sword against conspirators.
When think you that the sword goes up again? [25]
Never, till Caesar's three-and-thirty wounds
Be well avenged, or till another Caesar [26]
Have added slaughter to the sword of traitors.

BRUTUS.
Caesar, thou canst not die by traitors' hands,
Unless thou bring'st them with thee.

OCTAVIUS.
So I hope.
I was not born to die on Brutus' sword.

BRUTUS.
O, if thou wert the noblest of thy strain, [27]
Young man, thou couldst not die more honorable.

CASSIUS.
A peevish schoolboy, worthless of such honor, [28]
Joined with a masker and a reveler! [29]

ANTONY.
Old Cassius still.

OCTAVIUS.
Come, Antony, away!

---

25. up. in its sheath
26. till another ... traitors. until I, another Caesar, have
    also been killed by you
27. noblest ... strain. best of your family
28. peevish schoolboy. silly, childish. **worthless.**
    unworthy
29. masker ... reveler. one, like Antony, who takes part in
    masquerades and festivities

Defiance, traitors, hurl we in your teeth.
If you dare fight today, come to the field;
If not, when you have stomachs. [30]

[*Exit* OCTAVIUS, ANTONY, *and army*]

CASSIUS.
Why now, blow wind, swell billow, and swim bark! [31]
The storm is up, and all is on the hazard. [32]

BRUTUS.
Lo, Lucilius! Hark, a word with you.

LUCILIUS.
    [*Stands forth*]   My lord?

[BRUTUS *and* LUCILIUS *speak apart*]

CASSIUS.
Messala!

MESSALA.
    [*Stands forth*] What says my general?

CASSIUS.
                          Messala,
This is my birthday; as this very day [33]
Was Cassius born. Give me thy hand, Messala.
Be thou my witness that against my will,
As Pompey was, am I compelled to set [34]

---

30. **stomachs.** appetites for battle
31. **billow.** wave. **bark.** ship
32. **on the hazard.** at stake
33. **as.** on
34. **Pompey.** Against his own judgment, Pompey was urged
    to do battle against Caesar, which resulted in Pompey's
    defeat and death.

Upon one battle all our liberties.

You know that I held Epicurus strong [35]

And his opinion. Now I change my mind

And partly credit things that do presage. [36]

Coming from Sardis, on our former ensign [37]

Two mighty eagles fell, and there they perched, [38]

Gorging and feeding from our soldiers' hands,

Who to Philippi here consorted us. [39]

This morning are they fled away and gone,

And in their steads do ravens, crows, and kites [40]

Fly o'er our heads and downward look on us

As we were sickly prey. Their shadows seem [41]

A canopy most fatal, under which [42]

Our army lies, ready to give up the ghost.

MESSALA.

Believe not so.

CASSIUS.

I but believe it partly, [43]

For I am fresh of spirit and resolved

To meet all perils very constantly. [44]

---

35. held Epicurus strong. Cassius believed in Epicurus's
philosophy that the gods do not interest themselves in
human events and that omens are merely superstitions.
36. presage. foretell events
37. former ensign. foremost flag
38. fell. swooped down
39. consorted. accompanied
40. kites. birds of prey that are bad omens
41. As. as if
42. A canopy most fatal. a roof-like covering foretelling
death
43. but. only
44. very constantly. in a determined manner

BRUTUS.
Even so, Lucilius.

[*He rejoins* CASSIUS]

CASSIUS.
                    Now, most noble Brutus,
The gods today stand friendly, that we may, [45]
Lovers in peace, lead on our days to age! [46]
But since the affairs of men rest still incertain, [47]
Let's reason with the worst that may befall. [48]
If we do lose this battle, then is this
The very last time we shall speak together.
What are you then determinèd to do?

BRUTUS.
Even by the rule of that philosophy
By which I did blame Cato for the death [49]
Which he did give himself — I know not how,
But I do find it cowardly and vile,
For fear of what might fall, so to prevent [50]
The time of life — arming myself with patience
To stay the providence of some high powers [51]
That govern us below.

---

45. **The gods.** may the gods
46. **Lovers.** friends
47. **rest still.** always remain
48. **reason with.** consider. **befall.** happen
49. **Cato.** Marcus Porcius Cato, Brutus' father-in-law, who
    killed himself to avoid submission to Caesar in 46 B.C.
50. **so to prevent ... life.** thus to anticipate the natural end
    of life
51. **stay the providence.** await the fate

CASSIUS.

                        Then, if we lose this battle,
You are contented to be led in triumph [52]
Thorough the streets of Rome?

BRUTUS.

No, Cassius, no. Think not, thou noble Roman,
That ever Brutus will go bound to Rome;
He bears too great a mind. But this same day
Must end that work the ides of March begun.
And whether we shall meet again I know not;
Therefore our everlasting farewell take.
Forever and forever farewell, Cassius!
If we do meet again, why, we shall smile;
If not, why then this parting was well made.

CASSIUS.

Forever and forever farewell, Brutus!
If we do meet again, we'll smile indeed;
If not, 'tis true this parting was well made.

BRUTUS.

Why then, lead on. O, that a man might know
The end of this day's business ere it come!
But it sufficeth that the day will end,
And then the end is known. Come, ho, away!
                                      [Exit]

---

52. **in triumph.** as captive in the victor's procession

---◆---

Synopsis of Act V, Scene 1

Brutus's and Cassius's army met Antony's and Octavius's army at Philippi. Before the battle started, the leaders exchanged insults. Once alone, Brutus and Cassius bid each other farewell, sensing they would never see each other again.

---◆---

---◆---

Before You Read Act V, Scene 2

This scene takes place in a corner of the battlefield, and its purpose is to create a sense of the action that could not be shown on a small stage. Shakespeare purposely did not combine Scene 2 (which is only six lines long) with Scene 3. He wanted to help the audience imagine the large area in which the battle took place. As loud sounds of battle are heard in the background, Brutus gives Messala instructions to carry his written orders to Cassius's army. Brutus senses a lack of spirit in the enemy's army and predicts that a sudden attack will overthrow them. With what words does Brutus exit?

---◆---

ACT V. Scene 2.

Location: The plains of Philippi. The field of battle.

[*Alarum. Enter* BRUTUS *and* MESSALA] [1]

BRUTUS.
Ride, ride, Messala, ride, and give these bills [2]
Unto the legions on the other side. [3]

> [*He hands him written orders*]
> [*Loud alarum*]

Let them set on at once; for I perceive [4]
But cold demeanor in Octavius' wing, [5]
And sudden push gives them the overthrow. [6]
Ride, ride, Messala! Let them all come down. [7]

> [*Exit*]

---

1. **Alarum.** sounds, on or offstage, signifying battle
2. **bills.** written orders
3. **other side.** wing commanded by Cassius
4. **set on.** attack
5. **cold demeanor.** lack of spirit
6. **sudden push ... overthrow.** A sudden attack will defeat them.
7. **Let ... down.** Attack all at once from the hills.

---◆---

Synopsis of Act V, Scene 2

The previous brief scene depicted the beginning of battle. Brutus directed Messala to carry orders to Cassius. With sounds of battle in the background, Brutus sensed a weakness in Octavius's army.

---◆---

Before You Read Act V, Scene 3

This scene is a collection of brief episodes in the battle. Sounds of battle are heard in the background. Cassius tells Titinius that he had been forced to kill one of his own men who had "turned enemy." Notice that Titinius reports a mistake that Brutus had made. After Pindarus enters and reports that Mark Antony has burned their tents, Cassius sends his friend, Titinius, to check "whether yond troops are friend or enemy." Because Cassius has poor eyesight, he sends Pindarus to a higher hill to get a better view of Titinius. At this point Cassius feels he has lost the battle and gives up. Then Pindarus reports to Cassius that "Titinius is enclosed round about/With horsemen. . .He's ta'en! And, hark! They shout for joy." Notice how Cassius reacts to this news. What does he mean when he asks Pindarus to make himself "a free man"? What does he ask Pindarus to do?

Ironically, Messala was just about to bring Cassius the news that, even though Antony had defeated Cassius's army, Brutus had won over Octavius's army. Brutus enters and, upon viewing the death scene about him, mentions Caesar's spirit. Pay attention to what Brutus says Caesar's spirit has done. How does Brutus describe the two men whose bodies lie before him? Where does Brutus say they should be buried? Why?

ACT V. Scene 3.

Location: The plains of Philippi. The field of battle.

[*Alarums. Enter* CASSIUS, *carrying a standard, and* TITINIUS]

CASSIUS.
O, look, Titinius, look, the villains fly! [1]
Myself have to mine own turned enemy. [2]
This ensign here of mine was turning back; [3]
I slew the coward and did take it from him. [4]

TITINIUS.
O Cassius, Brutus gave the word too early,
Who, having some advantage on Octavius,
Took it too eagerly. His soldiers fell to spoil, [5]
Whilst we by Antony are all enclosed. [6]

[*Enter* PINDARUS]

PINDARUS.
Fly further off, my lord, fly further off!
Mark Antony is in your tents, my lord.
Fly therefore, noble Cassius, fly far off.

---

1. **the villains.** my own troops
2. **Myself ... enemy.** I have become an enemy to my own soldiers.
3. **ensign.** flag bearer
4. **it.** the ensign's flag
5. **fell to spoil.** began looting
6. **enclosed.** surrounded

CASSIUS.
 This hill is far enough. Look, look, Titinius:
 Are those my tents where I perceive the fire?

TITINIUS.
 They are, my lord.

CASSIUS.
     Titinius, if thou lovest me,
 Mount thou my horse and hide thy spurs in him
 Till he have brought thee up to yonder troops
 And here again, that I may rest assured
 Whether yond troops are friend or enemy.

TITINIUS.
 I will be here again even with a thought. [7]

             [Exit]

CASSIUS.
 Go, Pindarus, get higher on that hill.
 My sight was ever thick. Regard Titinius, [8]
 And tell me what thou not'st about the field.

        [Exit PINDARUS]

 This day I breathèd first. Time is come round, [9]
 And where I did begin, there shall I end.
 My life is run his compass. — Sirrah, what news? [10]

PINDARUS.
 [Above] O my lord!

---

7. **even ... thought.** as quick as a thought
8. **thick.** dim. **Regard.** observe
9. **breathèd first.** is my birthday
10. **his compass.** its full course

CASSIUS.
What news?

PINDARUS.
[*Above*]
Titinius is enclosèd round about
With horsemen that make to him on the spur, [11]
Yet he spurs on. Now they are almost on him.
Now, Titinius! Now some light. O, he [12]
Lights too. He's ta'en. [*Shout*] And hark! They
    shout for joy. [13]

CASSIUS.
Come down, behold no more.
O coward that I am, to live so long
To see my best friend ta'en before my face!

[*Enter* PINDARUS]

Come hither, sirrah.
In Parthia did I take thee prisoner,
And then I swore thee, saving of thy life, [14]
That whatsoever I did bid thee do
Thou shouldst attempt it. Come now, keep thine
    oath;
Now be a freeman, and with this good sword,
That ran through Caesar's bowels, search this
    bosom. [15]

---

11. **make ... spur.** ride toward him at top speed
12. **light.** dismount from their horses
13. **ta'en.** taken. Titinius has not been captured by enemy
    soldiers. He has been met by his own soldiers who have
    given him good news.
14. **swore ... of.** made you swear, when I spared
15. **search.** penetrate

Stand not to answer. Here, take thou the hilts, [16]
And when my face is covered, as 'tis now,
Guide thou the sword. — [PINDARUS *does so*]
    Caesar, thou art revenged,
Even with the sword that killed thee.

[*He dies*]

PINDARUS.
So, I am free, yet would not so have been [17]
Durst I have done my will. O Cassius! [18]
Far from this country Pindarus shall run,
Where never Roman shall take note of him.

[*Exit*]

[*Enter* TITINIUS, *with a garland of laurel, and* MESSALA]

MESSALA.
It is but change, Titinius; for Octavius [19]
Is overthrown by noble Brutus' power,
As Cassius' legions are by Antony.

TITINIUS.
These tidings will well comfort Cassius.

MESSALA.
Where did you leave him?

---

16. **Stand not.** do not wait.   **hilts.** sword handle
17. **so.** in this manner
18. **Durst.** dared
19. **change.** an exchange

TITINIUS.
                    All disconsolate,
With Pindarus his bondman, on this hill.

MESSALA.
Is not that he that lies upon the ground?

TITINIUS.
He lies not like the living. O my heart!

MESSALA.
Is not that he?

TITINIUS.
                    No, this was he, Messala,
But Cassius is no more. O setting sun,
As in thy red rays thou dost sink to night, [20]
So in his red blood Cassius' day is set!
The sun of Rome is set. Our day is gone; [21]
Clouds, dews, and dangers come; our deeds are
     done!
Mistrust of my success hath done this deed. [22]

MESSALA.
Mistrust of good success hath done this deed.
O hateful Error, Melancholy's child. [23]
Why dost thou show to the apt thoughts of men [24]

---

20. **to.** toward
21. **sun.** pun on "son"
22. **Mistrust.** Cassius' doubt
23. **hateful ... child.** Unhappiness is likely to cause
    mistakes.
24. **Why ... not?.** Why does error fill rational men with
    imagined fears?

The things that are not? O Error, soon conceived,
Thou never com'st unto a happy birth,
But kill'st the mother that engendered thee. [25]

TITINIUS.
What, Pindarus! Where art thou, Pindarus?

MESSALA.
Seek him, Titinius, whilst I go to meet
The noble Brutus, thrusting this report
Into his ears. I may say "thrusting" it;
For piercing steel and darts envenomèd [26]
Shall be as welcome to the ears of Brutus
As tidings of this sight.

TITINIUS.
Hie you, Messala, [27]
And I will seek for Pindarus the while.
[*Exit* MESSALA]

Why didst thou send me forth, brave Cassius?
Did I not meet thy friends? And did not they
Put on my brows this wreath of victory
And bid me give it thee? Didst thou not hear their
shouts?
Alas, thou hast misconstrued everything.
But, hold thee, take this garland on thy brow. [28]

[*He places a garland on* CASSIUS' *brow*]

---

25. mother ... thee. Cassius (in this case), who conceived
the error
26. darts. spears
27. Hie. hasten
28. hold thee. wait a moment

Thy Brutus bid me give it thee, and I
Will do his bidding. Brutus, come apace [29]
And see how I regarded Caius Cassius. [30]
By your leave, gods! This is a Roman's part. [31]
Come, Cassius' sword, and find Titinius' heart.

[He stabs himself and dies]

[Alarum. Enter BRUTUS, MESSALA, YOUNG
CATO, STRATO, VOLUMNIUS, *and* LUCILIUS,
LABEO, AND FLAVIUS]

BRUTUS.
Where, where, Messala, doth his body lie?

MESSALA.
Lo, yonder, and Titinius mourning it.

BRUTUS.
Titinius' face is upward.

CATO.
He is slain.

BRUTUS.
O Julius Caesar, thou art mighty yet!
Thy spirit walks abroad and turns our swords
In our own proper entrails. [32]

[Low alarums]

---

29. apace. quickly
30. regarded. honored
31. By your leave. with your permission.   **part.** role or
   duty
32. own proper entrails. very own inner organs

CATO.

Brave Titinius!

Look whe'er he have not crowned dead Cassius. [33]

BRUTUS.

Are yet two Romans living such as these?
The last of all the Romans, fare thee well!
It is impossible that ever Rome
Should breed thy fellow. Friends, I owe more tears
To this dead man than you shall see me pay. —
I shall find time, Cassius, I shall find time. —
Come, therefore, and to Thasos send his body. [34]
His funerals shall not be in our camp,
Lest it discomfort us. Lucilius, come, [35]
And come, young Cato, let us to the field.
Labeo and Flavius, set our battles on. [36]
'Tis three o'clock, and, Romans, yet ere night
We shall try fortune in a second fight.

[Exit] [37]

---

33. he have not crowned. he did crown
34. Thasos. an island not far from Philippi
35. discomfort us. discourage our soldiers
36. battles. armies
37. *Exit*. The bodies of Cassius and Titinius are carried off.

◆

Synopsis of Act V, Scene 3

Pindarus mistakenly thought that Titinius was being taken prisoner by Antony. Overcome with grief, Cassius asked Pindarus to take his sword (the sword with which he had killed Caesar) and kill him so that Caesar could be revenged. After Cassius died, Messala brought Brutus and the others in to see Cassius's body. Brutus commented in the same manner as Cassius, before he had died. Brutus said that Caesar's spirit was present and taking part in the war to seek revenge for his death. Titinius said that Cassius misunderstood what had happened, then stabbed himself with Cassius's sword. Brutus wanted the bodies to be buried far away so the troops would not be affected by the death of their leader.

◆

---◆---

Before You Read Act V, Scene 4

The short scene opens in one corner of the battlefield. Young Cato and Lucilius are fighting with enemy soldiers. Pay attention to how Lucilius tries to trick the soldiers while Brutus gets away. How is Cato related to Brutus? Notice Cato's words that describe his allegiance to Rome. Lucilius tries to persuade the enemy soldiers to kill him, but he is taken prisoner instead. Think about why Antony wants Lucilius to be treated kindly.

---◆---

ACT V. Scene 4.

Location: The field of battle.

[*Alarum.   Enter* BRUTUS, MESSALA, YOUNG CATO, LUCILIUS, *and* FLAVIUS]

BRUTUS.
Yet, countrymen, O, yet hold up your heads!

[*Exit, followed by* MESSALA *and* FLAVIUS]

CATO.
What bastard doth not? Who will go with me? [1]
I will proclaim my name about the field:
I am the son of Marcus Cato, ho! [2]
A foe to tyrants, and my country's friend.
I am the son of Marcus Cato, ho!

[*Enter soldiers, and fight*]

LUCILIUS.
And I am Brutus, Marcus Brutus, I
Brutus, my country's friend! Know me for Brutus!

[YOUNG CATO *is slain by* ANTONY'S *men*]

O young and noble Cato, art thou down?
Why, now thou diest as bravely as Titinius,
And mayst be honored, being Cato's son.

FIRST SOLDIER.
[*Capturing* LUCILIUS]
Yield, or thou diest.

---

1. **What ... not.** What person is not a true Roman?
2. **Marcus Cato.** Brutus's wife's father

LUCILIUS.
> [*Offering money*] Only I yield to die. [3]
> There is so much that thou wilt kill me straight; [4]
> Kill Brutus, and be honored in his death.

FIRST SOLDIER.
> We must not. A noble prisoner!

SECOND SOLDIER.
> Room, ho! Tell Antony, Brutus is ta'en.

[*Enter* ANTONY]

FIRST SOLDIER.
> I'll tell the news. Here comes the General.
> Brutus is ta'en, Brutus is ta'en, my lord.

ANTONY.
> Where is he?

LUCILIUS.
> Safe, Antony, Brutus is safe enough.
> I dare assure thee that no enemy
> Shall ever take alive the noble Brutus.
> The gods defend him from so great a shame!
> When you do find him, or alive or dead, [5]
> He will be found like Brutus, like himself. [6]

---

3. **Only ... die.** I will surrender only to die.
4. **There ... straight.** Here is money for you to kill me at once.
5. **or alive.** either alive
6. **like himself.** behaving in a noble way

ANTONY.

[*To* FIRST SOLDIER]

This is not Brutus, friend, but, I assure you,
A prize no less in worth. Keep this man safe;
Give him all kindness. I had rather have
Such men my friends than enemies. Go on,
And see whe'er Brutus be alive or dead; [7]
And bring us word unto Octavius' tent
How everything is chanced. [8]

[*Exit separately*] [9]

---

7. whe'er. whether
8. is chanced. has happened
9. *Exit.* The body of Young Cato is carried off at this point.

————————◆————————

Synopsis of Act V, Scene 4

In this brief scene, Lucilius and Cato engaged in hand-to-hand combat with enemy soldiers so that Brutus could escape. Cato pledged his allegiance to Rome and Lucilius tried to trick the soldiers into killing him by telling them that he was Brutus. Instead, he was taken prisoner. Antony recognized Lucilius and told the soldiers to treat him well.

————————◆————————

---◆---

Before You Read Act V, Scene 5

Brutus's scout, Statilius, sets out to locate the position of the enemy, but he does not return. Brutus senses defeat. He sits on a rock with his servants, Clitus and Dardanius. He makes a request of them, but they refuse. Brutus tells Volumnius that Caesar's ghost appeared to him once again, here, in Philippi. The appearance of Caesar's ghost has a special meaning for Brutus. Notice what he wants Volumnius to do. In Brutus's farewell to his friends he gives his reasons for wanting to die. Pay attention to the words that give his reasons for wanting to die. Pay special attention to Brutus's dying words to Caesar.

Octavius rides up with Messala and Lucilius, who both have been taken prisoner. Strato tells them how Brutus has died and Octavius takes Brutus's men into his service. Then Antony gives a moving eulogy over Brutus's body. Does Antony portray Brutus as the tragic hero? Why? Why not?

---◆---

ACT V. Scene 5.

Location: The field of battle still.

[*Enter* BRUTUS, DARDANIUS, CLITUS,
STRATO, *and* VOLUMNIUS]

BRUTUS.
Come, poor remains of friends, rest on this rock. [1]

[*He sits*]

CLITUS.
Statilius showed the torchlight, but, my lord, [2]
He came not back. He is or ta'en or slain. [3]

BRUTUS.
Sit thee down, Clitus. Slaying is the word.
It is a deed in fashion. Hark thee, Clitus.

[*He whispers*]

CLITUS.
What, I, my lord? No, not for all the world.

BRUTUS.
Peace then. No words.

CLITUS.
I'll rather kill myself.

BRUTUS.
Hark thee, Dardanius.

[*He whispers*]

---

1. **poor remains.** pitiful survivors
2. **Statilius ... torchlight.** Brutus's scout, Statilius, has
    signaled with a torchlight.
3. **or ta'en** either taken

DARDANIUS
Shall I do such a deed?

[DARDANIUS *and* CLITUS *move away from* BRUTUS]

CLITUS.
O Dardanius!

DARDANIUS
O Clitus!

CLITUS.
What ill request did Brutus make to thee?

DARDANIUS
To kill him, Clitus. Look, he meditates.

CLITUS.
Now is that noble vessel full of grief,
That it runs over even at his eyes.

BRUTUS.
Come hither, good Volumnius. List a word. [4]

VOLUMNIUS.
What says my lord?

BRUTUS.
Why, this, Volumnius:
The ghost of Caesar hath appeared to me
Two several times by night — at Sardis once, [5]

---

4. **List.** hear
5. **several.** separate

And this last night here in Philippi fields.
I know my hour is come.

VOLUMNIUS.

> Not so, my lord.

BRUTUS.

Nay, I am sure it is, Volumnius.
Thou seest the world, Volumnius, how it goes;
Our enemies have beat us to the pit. [6]

> *[Low alarums]*

It is more worthy to leap in ourselves
Than tarry till they push us. Good Volumnius,
Thou know'st that we two went to school together.
Even for that, our love of old, I prithee, [7]
Hold thou my sword hilts whilst I run on it. [8]

VOLUMNIUS.

That's not an office for a friend, my lord. [9]

> *[Alarum still]*

CLITUS.

Fly, fly, my lord! There is no tarrying here.

BRUTUS.

Farewell to you, and you, and you, Volumnius.
Strato, thou hast been all this while asleep;
Farewell to thee too, Strato. Countrymen,
My heart doth joy that yet in all my life

---

6. **beat.** driven. **pit.** grave
7. **love of old.** long-time friendship
8. **hilts.** by the handle
9. **office.** duty

I found no man but he was true to me.
I shall have glory by this losing day
More than Octavius and Mark Antony
By this vile conquest shall attain unto. [10]
So fare you well at once, for Brutus' tongue [11]
Hath almost ended his life's history.
Night hangs upon mine eyes; my bones would rest,
That have but labored to attain this hour. [12]

> [*Alarum. Cry within,* "Fly, fly, fly!"]

CLITUS.
Fly, my lord, fly!

BRUTUS.
                    Hence, I will follow.

[*Exit* CLITUS, DARDANIUS, *and* VOLUMNIUS]

I prithee, Strato, stay thou by thy lord.
Thou art a fellow of a good respect; [13]
Thy life hath had some smatch of honor in it. [14]
Hold then my sword, and turn away thy face,
While I do run upon it. Wilt thou, Strato?

STRATO.
Give me your hand first. Fare you well, my lord.

---

10. **By this ... unto.** by this evil victory shall gain (Brutus
    sees the victory of Antony and Octavius as causing the
    downfall of Rome.)
11. **at once.** all together
12. **to ... hour.** to reach this moment of death
13. **respect.** reputation
14. **some smatch.** a touch

BRUTUS.
Farewell, good Strato. [*He runs on his sword*]
    Caesar, now be still.
I killed not thee with half so good a will.

[*Dies*]

[*Alarum. Retreat. Enter* ANTONY, OCTAVIUS;
MESSALA, LUCILIUS *as prisoners; and the army*]

OCTAVIUS.
What man is that?

MESSALA.
My master's man. Strato, where is thy master? [15]

STRATO.
Free from the bondage you are in, Messala.
The conquerors can but make a fire of him,
For Brutus only overcame himself, [16]
And no man else hath honor by his death. [17]

LUCILIUS.
So Brutus should be found. I thank thee, Brutus,
That thou hast proved Lucilius' saying true. [18]

OCTAVIUS.
All that served Brutus, I will entertain them. [19]
Fellow, wilt thou bestow thy time with me?

---

15. **man.** servant
16. **Brutus ... himself.** only Brutus conquered Brutus
17. **no ... honor.** no other man gains honor (by Brutus's
    death)
18. **That ... true.** See Act V, Scene 4, line 25.
19. **entertain them.** take them into my service

STRATO.
Ay, if Messala will prefer me to you. [20]

OCTAVIUS.
Do so, good Messala.

MESSALA.
How died my master, Strato?

STRATO.
I held the sword, and he did run on it.

MESSALA.
Octavius, then take him to follow thee, [21]
That did the latest service to my master. [22]

ANTONY.
This was the noblest Roman of them all.
All the conspirators save only he [23]
Did that they did in envy of great Caesar; [24]
He only in a general honest thought
And common good to all made one of them. [25]
His life was gentle, and the elements [26]
So mixed in him that Nature might stand up [27]
And say to all the world, "This was a man!"

---

20. **prefer.** recommend
21. **follow.** serve
22. **latest.** last
23. **save.** except
24. **that.** what. **in envy of.** malice toward
25. **made one of them.** became one of the conspirators
26. **gentle.** noble.
27. **mixed.** well-balanced.

OCTAVIUS.
  According to his virtue let us use him, [28]
  With all respect and rites of burial.
  Within my tent his bones tonight shall lie,
  Most like a soldier, ordered honorably. [29]
  So call the field to rest, and let's away [30]
  To part the glories of this happy day. [31]

                    [*Exit all with* BRUTUS' *body*]

---

28. virtue. excellence
29. ordered. treated
30. field. army
31. part. share

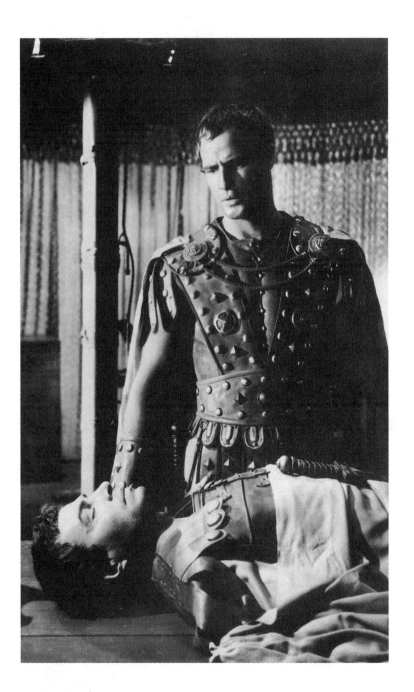

◆

Synopsis of Act V, Scene 5

This final scene resolves the last remaining conflict in the play. Assuming that his scout had been taken prisoner or slain by the enemy when he did not return to camp, Brutus sensed the defeat of his army. Then, wanting to die, Brutus asked Clitus and Dardanius if they would assist in carrying out his wishes, but they would not. Then he turned to Volumnius and made a similar request, adding that the ghost of Caesar had visited him the previous night. Brutus bid his loyal friends farewell and, after a warning, they all fled except Strato. Brutus then asked Strato to hold his sword so that he could run upon it. Strato reluctantly carried out his request. After Brutus died, Octavius entered and took Brutus's men into his service. The play ended with a eulogy given by Mark Antony over Brutus's body and Octavius's promise to give Brutus a proper soldier's funeral.

◆

REVIEWING

YOUR

READING

Act I, Scene 1

FINDING THE MAIN IDEA

1. This opening scene of the play is mostly about the conflict between
   (A) Flavius and Marullus   (B) the cobbler and Marullus
   (C) the tribunes and the commoners   (D) Flavius and the carpenter

REMEMBERING DETAILS

2. The commoners are dressed in their best clothes to celebrate
   (A) Caesar's victory over Pompey's sons   (B) the festival of Lupercal   (C) both A and B   (D) not A or B

3. What words does Marullus use to describe the cobbler's behavior?
   (A) he says the cobbler is a "naughty knave"   (B) he calls the cobbler a "saucy fellow"   (C) he says the cobbler is an "idle creature"   (D) he thinks the cobbler is a "good countryman"

4. The tribunes order the commoners to go home and
   (A) pray to the gods   (B) rest   (C) go back to work   (D) wait for Caesar's return

5. Marullus says the "ingratitude" of the people will result in
   (A) civil war   (B) giant floods   (C) a plague of misfortune   (D) longer work hours for the people

DRAWING CONCLUSIONS

6. The cobbler's words to Flavius, "sir, I can mend you" show
   (A) that he is a good worker   (B) that he wants to work during this holiday   (C) the tension between the two classes   (D) his sense of humor

7. When Marullus asks, "What tributaries follow him to Rome. . .," he is referring to
   (A) money not brought by Pompey into Rome
   (B) money not brought into Rome by Caesar   (C) rivers running into Rome (D) prisoners captured by Caesar

8. After the commoners leave, Flavius and Marullus
   (A) attend the feast of Lupercal   (B) rejoice
   (C) remove garlands from around the necks of statues of
   Caesar   (D) kneel and pray

USING YOUR REASON

9. You can figure out from this scene that if Caesar
   becomes more powerful,
   (A) he will deny the people their rights   (B) he will take
   away power from the tribunes   (C) he will win
   additional victories for Rome   (D) he will change the
   labor laws

IDENTIFYING THE MOOD

10. What mood does this opening scene create?
    (A) excitement   (B) horror   (C) tension   (D) suspense

THINKING IT OVER

1. As Flavius removes garlands from the statues of Caesar,
   he says, "These growing feathers plucked from Caesar's
   wing/Will make him fly an ordinary pitch. . . ." What
   does he mean? What do these words tell about his
   predictions for Caesar? Explain your answer.
2. In this scene, Flavius and Marullus scold the people for
   shifting their loyalty from Pompey to Caesar. Is loyalty
   their real concern or are they just being selfish? Explain
   your answer.
3. Notice that the tribunes speak in blank verse and the
   commoners speak in prose. What is Shakespeare's
   purpose in using a different style of language for each
   class?

Act I, Scene 2

FINDING THE MAIN IDEA

1. The most important event that takes place in this scene is
(A) Caesar becomes suspicious of Cassius   (B) Cassius
successfully convinces Brutus to lead the conspiracy
(C) Cassius writes letters and will have them delivered to
Brutus   (D) Mark Antony runs the traditional race
during the festival of Lupercal

REMEMBERING DETAILS

2. With what words does Caesar respond to the soothsayer's
warning to him to "beware the ides of March"?
(A) "Speak; Caesar is turned to hear"   (B) "He is a
dreamer, let us leave him. Pass."   (C) "Bid every noise
be still;"   (D) "Set on, and leave no ceremony out."

3. When Antony offered Caesar the crown,
(A) Caesar refused it each time   (B) the crowd shouted
for Caesar to take it   (C) Caesar finally accepted it after
the third time   (D) Brutus stopped the ceremony

4. According to Cassius, what is Brutus's worth compared
to Caesar's?
(A) Caesar's worth is a great deal more   (B) Brutus's
worth is a great deal more   (C) Brutus and Caesar are of
equal worth   (D) Brutus's worth is a great deal less than
Caesar's

5. Brutus shows that he is interested in what Cassius has
been saying about Caesar by
(A) inviting Cassius to his house   (B) inviting Casca to
"sup" with him   (C) agreeing that Caesar has "falling-
sickness"   (D) speaking with Cicero himself

DRAWING CONCLUSIONS

6. When Brutus says, "Vexéd I am/Of late with passions of
some difference," he is probably troubled about
(A) the success of the feast   (B) the soothsayer's health
(C) Caesar's latest victory   (D) the tribunes' treatment
of the people

7. When Caesar says, "Yond Cassius has a lean and hungry look," he means that
(A) Cassius is too thin   (B) Cassius will be a good friend to him   (C) Cassius should eat something at the festival   (D) Cassius will somehow be a danger to him

USING YOUR REASON

8. Why is Brutus interested in finding out what caused the crowd to shout?
(A) he needs to report back to the senate   (B) he is jealous of Caesar's popularity   (C) he wants to know if Caesar has the support of the people   (D) he wishes he could participate in the festivities

9. The real reason Cassius hates Caesar and wants him killed is probably that
(A) he fears what will happen to Rome if Caesar becomes the ruler   (B) he is a shrewd, ambitious man who is jealous of Caesar's power   (C) he feels that Caesar does not have honest intentions for Rome
(D) none of the above

THINKING IT OVER

1. What are Brutus's reasons for agreeing that Caesar must be killed? Compare Brutus's motives with Cassius's. Is one man being more honorable than the other? Explain your opinion.

2. In Cassius's soliloquy at the end of the scene, he uses the words noble and honorable to describe Brutus. Do you think he might be using these words ironically? Explain your answer.

Act I, Scene 3

FINDING THE MAIN IDEA

1. The main purpose of this scene is for Cassius to find out
(A) what has caused the storm   (B) if Casca is
committed to the conspiracy   (C) if Cicero is a
conspirator   (D) Casca's plans for the conspiracy

REMEMBERING DETAILS

2. This scene takes place
(A) in the Roman hills   (B) on a Roman street
(C) a year later   (D) in the early morning hours

3. When Cassius says, "Now could I, Casca, name to thee a
man/Most like this dreadful night," he is referring to
(A) Casca   (B) Cicero   (C) Pompey   (D) Caesar

4. What is Cassius prepared to do if Caesar is crowned the
next day?
(A) deliver the letters himself   (B) kill Casca   (C) kill
Caesar   (D) kill himself

DRAWING CONCLUSIONS

5. Casca is upset because
(A) Cicero is out late at night   (B) he sees many
unnatural things in the storm   (C) Cassius does not
agree with the storm's warnings   (D) Cinna has been
asked to deliver the letters

USING YOUR REASON

6. Cassius cleverly compares the unnatural events in the
storm to Caesar's unnatural power
(A) to get Cicero to leave   (B) to find out if Casca is
committed to the conspiracy   (C) to test Casca's
knowledge of the supernatural   (D) in order to confuse
the gods

7. These words spoken by Casca, "So can I;/So every bondman in his own hand bears/The power to cancel his captivity" reveal that Casca feels
(A) everyone who opposes Caesar should be imprisoned
(B) he has the power to do something about Caesar's possible tyryanny   (C) he should be imprisoned
(D) anyone in prison should have a plan to free himself

IDENTIFYING THE MOOD
8. In this scene, Casca is
(A) overjoyed   (B) calm   (C) happy   (D) terrified

THINKING IT OVER
1. What does this scene tell you about Cassius's true nature? Use some examples from the play to explain your answer.
2. What effect does Shakespeare intend the storm to have in this scene? Do Casca's, Cassius's and Cicero's conflicting views of the storm reflect the conflicts in Rome? How? Explain your answer.

Act II, Scene 1

FINDING THE MAIN IDEA
1. The main conflict at the beginning of this scene involves
   (A) Caesar's love for Rome and his desire for the crown
   (B) Brutus's love for Caesar and his loyalty to Rome
   (C) Brutus and the conspirators   (D) Brutus and Cassius

REMEMBERING DETAILS
2. Due to this great internal conflict, Brutus
   (A) drinks too much wine   (B) sleeps long hours
   (C) becomes violent   (D) is restless and cannot sleep
3. The conspirators visit Brutus
   (A) on their way to the Capitol   (B) to find out if he has
   received Cassius's forged letters   (C) to plan the
   assassination   (D) to bring greetings to Portia
4. Who says that he will make sure Caesar arrives at the
   Capitol?
   (A) Lucius   (B) Cinna   (C) Metellus   (D) Decius
5. What does Brutus's wife, Portia, do to show her "strong
   proof of my constancy" toward Brutus?
   (A) she gives herself a voluntary wound   (B) she kneels
   and says "and upon my knees/I charm you,"   (C) she
   leaves the room   (D) she agrees to go with Brutus to the
   Capitol

DRAWING CONCLUSIONS
6. The words, ". . .it sufficeth/That Brutus leads me on,"
   spoken by Caius Ligarus, show
   (A) that the people fear Brutus   (B) that the people of
   Rome hold Brutus in high regard   (C) that Brutus is not
   strong enough to lead the others   (D) none of the above
7. Which words spoken by Brutus show that he had mixed
   feelings about the conspiracy to kill Caesar?
   (A) "I know no personal harm to spurn at him"   (B) "He
   would be crowned./How that might change his nature,"
   (C) "And therefore think him as a serpent's egg"
   (D) all of the above

USING YOUR REASON

8. You can figure out from this scene that Brutus is allowed to take the leadership of the conspiracy because (A) he is very clever politically   (B) the other conspirators fear for their lives if they don't   (C) Brutus is their friend   (D) the conspirators assume that the people of Rome will support them if this honorable man and loyal friend to Caesar is their leader

9. The fact that Brutus does not want to kill Mark Antony along with Caesar reveals that Brutus is (A) noble-minded in his views   (B) cautious politically (C) naturally blood-thirsty and violent   (D) a good friend of Mark Antony's

THINKING IT OVER

1. Brutus's position in the conspiracy is established in this scene. Does he take the position of a leader or a follower? Give at least three examples to explain your answer.

2. Caesar says that he is unmoved by flattery, but actually this is not so. How does Decius make this point about Caesar?

3. Have you ever used flattery to convince someone to do something? Give some examples.

Act II, Scene 2

FINDING THE MAIN IDEA

1. This scene is mostly about
   (A) Calpurnia's recurring dream   (B) the relationship between Caesar and Calpurnia   (C) Caesar's decision whether or not to attend the Senate   (D) the augurers

REMEMBERING DETAILS

2. What does Calpurnia call out in her sleep?
   (A) "Beware the ides of March, Caesar"   (B) "Help, ho! They murder Caesar!"   (C) "Break up the Senate"
   (D) "Fierce fiery warriors fought upon the clouds"
3. Caesar changes his mind about going to the Senate
   (A) after Decius says they will offer Caesar the crown
   (B) after Decius reinterprets Calpurnia's dream
   (C) after Decius says that Caesar would appear weak to listen to his wife   (D) all of the above
4. What do the augurers, or interpreters of omens, not find in the animal they have sacrificed?
   (A) a heart   (B) teeth   (C) a tongue   (D) a tail
5. Not finding this important organ is
   (A) a good omen   (B) not significant   (C) a bad omen
   (D) highly unlikely

DRAWING CONCLUSIONS

6. With the words, "Your statue spouting blood.../Signifies that from you great Rome shall suck/Reviving blood...", Decius is
   (A) reciting poetry   (B) talking about Pompey
   (C) reinterpreting Calpurnia's dream   (D) none of the above
7. In the quote above, Decius is
   (A) playing on Caesar's desire to become ruler of Rome
   (B) trying to convince Caesar to attend the Senate
   (C) both A and B   (D) neither A nor B

USING YOUR REASON

8. Trebonius's aside, "and so near will I be,/That your best friends shall wish I had been further,"
   (A) is meant to distract Caesar   (B) refers to the plot to kill Caesar   (C) is spoken to Antony   (D) speaks of his respect for Caesar

THINKING IT OVER

1. Think about the different ways that Caesar behaves in this scene. What does his disregard of Calpurnia's dream tell you about him? Has he responded similarly to other warnings? Is it like Caesar to ask for the augurer's findings from the animal sacrifice? Why do you think he then disregarded the augurer's warnings?

2. What does Caesar mean when he says, "Cowards die many times before their deaths;/The valiant never taste of death but once."? How do these lines reflect Caesar's inner conflict? Do you agree or disagree with this statement? Explain your opinion.

Act II, Scene 3

FINDING THE MAIN IDEA

1. The main purpose of this scene is to
   (A) allow time for Caesar to travel to the Capitol
   (B) heighten the suspense in the play   (C) reveal that
   there are others who are aware of the plot   (D) show
   that Artemidorus was among the conspirators

REMEMBERING DETAILS

2. Artemidorus is waiting for Caesar
   (A) to warn him about the plot   (B) to hand him the note
   (C) both A and B   (D) neither A nor B
3. The note Artemidorus is reading consists of
   (A) a diagram   (B) a secret message   (C) omens and
   prophesies   (D) the conspirators' names and their
   purpose

DRAWING CONCLUSIONS

4. Which words spoken by Artemidorus warn Caesar that
   he may be acting too confidently?
   (A) "beware of Brutus"   (B) "Here I will stand till
   Caesar pass along,"   (C) "If thou read this, O Caesar,
   thou mayest live;"   (D) "security gives way to
   conspiracy."
5. The word "suitor" implies that Artemidorus is Caesar's
   (A) enemy   (B) brother   (C) tailor   (D) friend

THINKING IT OVER

Do you think Caesar will read Artemidorus's note? If he
does read it, how do you think he will respond? Explain
your opinion.

Act II, Scene 4

FINDING THE MAIN IDEA

1. The main purpose of this scene is to
   (A) reintroduce Portia into the play   (B) reintroduce the soothsayer into the play   (C) bring Lucius back into the action   (D) none of the above

REMEMBERING DETAILS

2. Why does Portia send Lucilius to the Capitol?
   (A) to find Mark Antony   (B) to fetch the soothsayer
   (C) to tell Caesar that the soothsayer is waiting to speak to him   (D) to find out how Brutus looks and who is with Caesar
3. At what time does this scene take place?
   (A) early morning   (B) eight o'clock   (C) nine o'clock
   (D) noon
4. The soothsayer says that he will
   (A) stay among the crowd   (B) find a narrower street
   (C) go back home   (D) stand where there are fewer people

DRAWING CONCLUSIONS

5. Which words express the main purpose of Portia's conversation with the soothsayer?
   (A) "Which way hast thou been?"   (B) "Is Caesar yet gone to the Capitol?"   (C) "What is't o'clock?"
   (D) "know'st thou any harm's intended towards him?"

USING YOUR REASON

6. You can figure out from this scene between Portia and the soothsayer that Portia is mostly concerned
   (A) about whether or not word of the conspiracy has gotten out   (B) with how Brutus is feeling   (C) whether there will be enough time for the conspirators to gather together   (D) about her own strength as a woman

THINKING IT OVER

1. Compare the personalities of Caesar and Brutus so far in the play. How does this portrayal of Caesar influence the audience's reaction to the conspiracy? Do you sympathize more with Caesar or Brutus?
2. Rather than joining the conspiracy, what else might Brutus have done to save Rome from Caesar's possible political tyranny? Do you agree with his decision? Do you think he was being truly honorable? Explain your opinion.

Act III, Scene 1

1. The most important thing that happens in this scene is
   (A) Caesar ignores the soothsayer (B) Antony flees
   (C) Caesar is attacked (D) Artemidorus approaches

1. Who is first to mention that the ides of March has arrived?
   (A) the soothsayer (B) Brutus (C) Caesar
   (D) Artemidorus
2. What happens when Artemidorus tries to hand Caesar his document?
   (A) Caesar turns away to talk to the soothsayer (B) Artimodorus trips on a step (C) Decius pushes forward with a paper and Publius pushes Artemidorus aside (D) Caesar takes the note and reads it
3. At the beginning of the scene, who do the conspirators fear will tell Caesar about their plan?
   (A) Cassius (B) Brutus (C) Metellus (D) Popilius
4. Antony compares Caesar to a slain
   (A) sheep (B) lion (C) god (D) deer
5. Cassius and Brutus disagree about
   (A) what to do with Mark Antony (B) which of them should give Caesar's funeral speech (C) whether or not to allow Mark Antony to give the funeral speech
   (D) who will now lead Rome

6. You can conclude that the conspirators have planned carefully for the time just before the assassination when (A) Popilius goes to speak with Caesar (B) Mark Antony gives his long speech (C) Metellus petitions Caesar to forgive his brother (D) Brutus kisses Caesar's hand

7. You can figure out that the conspirators did not predict what might happen after the killing
   (A) because there is total chaos among the senators
   (B) the senators listen to Cinna and cry out "Liberty! Freedom! Tyranny is dead!"   (C) the conspirators themselves flee   (D) Antony flees to his house

USING YOUR REASON

8. When Caesar says, "*Et tu, Brutè?* Then fall Caesar." he is referring to
   (A) his love for Brutus   (B) his betrayal by Brutus
   (C) this unexpected death blow   (D) all of the above

9. Brutus tries to portray the assassination as an almost glorious, sacrificial act by asking the conspirators to
   (A) stay nearby and hear Antony's words   (B) not kill Antony   (C) kill themselves   (D) wash their hands in Caesar's blood

THINKING IT OVER

1. Do you think Antony should speak at the funeral? Has Antony already shown that he may be dangerous to the conspirators? What is it about Brutus that keeps him from seeing the danger Antony poses?

2. How does the arrival of Octavius, Caesar's nephew and heir, create a new conflict in the play and change the direction of the action? Who will this conflict involve? What do you think the outcome will be?

Act III, Scene 2

FINDING THE MAIN IDEA

1. This scene is mostly concerned with
   (A) Brutus's feelings of guilt   (B) Cassius's fear for his
   life   (C) Antony's plan for revenge   (D) the reaction of
   the people to Caesar's death

REMEMBERING DETAILS

2. When Brutus says, "Not that I loved Caesar less, but that
   I loved Rome more" he is referring to
   (A) the reason he joined the conspiracy   (B) the reason
   he agreed that Caesar should be killed   (C) both A and
   B   (D) neither A nor B

3. At first, the commoners, or plebeians, are calm when
   Brutus speaks and call out
   (A) "Live, Brutus! Live!"   (B) "Bring him with triumph
   home unto his house."   (C) "Give him a statue with his
   ancestors."   (D) all of the above

4. "Friends, Romans, countrymen, lend me your ears;/I
   come to bury Caesar, not to praise him"
   (A) are the opening words in Brutus's speech   (B) are
   the opening words in Antony's speech   (C) are spoken
   as the third plebeian prepares Caesar's burial plot
   (D) none of the above

5. What did Caesar leave the people in his will?
   (A) five drachmas and the use of his house
   (B) seventy-five drachmas and the use of his walks,
   arbors, and orchards   (C) only seventy-five drachmas
   (D) only the use of his orchards

6. After hearing Antony's eloquent speech, the crowd
   (A) shifts its support to Antony   (B) seeks revenge for
   Caesar's death   (C) takes up Caesar's body and
   disperses to torch the conspirators' houses   (D) all of
   the above

DRAWING CONCLUSIONS

7. You can figure out that by repeatedly calling attention to Brutus as "an honorable man," Antony
   (A) wants to build up the conspirators in the minds of the people (B) honestly feels Brutus performed an honorable act (C) really wants the crowd to think that Brutus is dishonorable (D) wants to contrast how he feels about Brutus with how he feels about Cassius

8. Which words spoken by Antony are intended to manipulate the crowd?
   (A) "Good friends, sweet friends, let me not stir you up" (B) "I am no orator, as Brutus is;" (C) "...But were I Brutus,/And Brutus Antony" (D) all of the above

USING YOUR REASON

9. What might the conspirators do now that the people have turned against them and side with Antony?
   (A) surrender (B) return to their homes (C) kill themselves (D) create their own armies

THINKING IT OVER

1. Notice that Shakespeare has written Brutus's speech in prose but Antony's speech is written in blank verse. What was Shakespeare's purpose in doing this?

2. What do you think you would have done if you were in Brutus's place? Have you ever had to choose between a friend and a higher principle? Describe your experience.

Act III, Scene 3

FINDING THE MAIN IDEA

1. The main purpose of this scene is to show
    (A) how poor the lighting was on Shakespeare's stage
    (B) the dangers of two people having the same name
    (C) the power of the mob after Caesar's death
    (D) Shakespeare's opinion of poets

REMEMBERING DETAILS

2. Who does Cinna dream that he is feasting with?
    (A)   Antony   (B) Brutus   (C) Calpurnia   (D) Caesar
3. Where is Cinna headed?
    (A) home   (B) to Caesar's funeral   (C) home from
    Caesar's funeral   (D) to Antony's house

DRAWING CONCLUSIONS

4. Shakespeare seems to be poking fun at bad poets when
    the Fourth Plebeian says,
    (A) "Where do you dwell?"   (B) "As a friend or an
    enemy?"   (C) "Whither are you going?"   (D) "Tear
    him for his bad verses!"

USING YOUR REASON

5. Cinna's dream at the beginning of this scene,
    (A) indicates that he is late for the funeral   (B) shows
    that he was a good friend of Caesar's   (C) foreshadows
    what happens to him later in the scene   (D) is probably
    the result of eating too much

THINKING IT OVER

Shakespeare often uses staging to highlight themes in the
play. Describe what the stage might look like in this
scene so that it would reflect the mood in Rome at this
time.

Act IV, Scene 1

FINDING THE MAIN IDEA

1. This scene is mostly concerned with
   (A) whom the triumvirs decide to kill   (B) how Lepidus will get Caesar's will   (C) how corrupt the power in Rome has become   (D) how the triumvirs are getting along

REMEMBERING DETAILS

2. Antony has joined forces with
   (A) the triumvirs   (B) Lepidus and Octavius
   (C) Octavius   (D) Lucilius
3. Antony wants to dismiss
   (A) Octavius   (B) Lepidus   (C) both A and B
   (D) neither A nor B
4. Antony sends Lepidus to
   (A) find Cassius and Brutus   (B) steal money from the people   (C) get Caesar's will   (D) spy on Octavius

DRAWING CONCLUSIONS

5. When Antony says, "Brutus and Cassius/Are levying powers; we must straight make head," he is talking about his urgent need to
   (A) cut off money from the people   (B) show the people who is in charge   (C) gather together an army
   (D) none of the above

USING YOUR REASON

6. You can figure out that Antony wants to take the money from the people and use it to
   (A) pay off Lepidus   (B) pay off Brutus and Cassius
   (C) pay for his army   (D) demonstrate his power
7. By not wanting to share power with Lepidus, Antony is
   (A) being very clever   (B) being very cautious
   (C) showing his corrupt nature   (D) showing his jealousy

8. The shift in setting from the streets of Rome to Antony's house reflects the shift in power
   (A) away from the commoners   (B) to Octavius
   (C) to the conspirators   (D) to Antony

THINKING IT OVER

How does Octavius respond when Antony suggests that they dismiss Lepidus? What does Octavius's response tell you about him? How does Octavius seem to be reacting to Antony as this scene ends? From this scene can you make a prediction about the the future of the triumvir's rule?

Act IV, Scene 2

FINDING THE MAIN IDEA

1. The purpose of this scene is to inform the audience
   (A) that Brutus has lost respect for Cassius   (B) of the
   fighting that has begun between the conspirators
   (C) both A and B   (D) neither A nor B

REMEMBERING DETAILS

2. This scene takes place
   (A) on a street in Rome   (B) several years later
   (C) at a military camp near Sardis   (D) after Octavius
   has become the ruler of Rome

3. In order to find out how Cassius feels about Brutus,
   (A) Brutus wrote Cassius a note asking his feelings
   (B) Brutus asks his servant, Lucilius, how Cassius
   treated him   (C) Brutus invited Cassius to his camp
   (D) none of the above

4. When Brutus asks Lucilius how he was received by
   Cassius, Lucilius responds,
   (A) "With courtesy and with respect enough,"   (B) "But
   not with such familiar instances,"   (C) "Nor with such
   free and friendly conference/As he hath used of old."
   (D) all of the above

DRAWING CONCLUSIONS

5. When Pindarus says that his master is still "full of regard
   and honor," he is referring to
   (A) Brutus's feelings toward Cassius   (B) Cassius's
   feelings toward Brutus   (C) Cassius's feelings toward
   his servant   (D) Brutus's feelings toward Octavius

USING YOUR REASON

6. Brutus, once again, questions his own decision to kill
   Caesar when he says,
   (A) "He greets me well. Your master, Pindarus"
   (B) "Stand ho!"   (C) ". . . Hath given me some worthy
   cause to wish/Things done undone;"   (D) "He is not
   doubted."

THINKING IT OVER

1. How does Brutus respond when Cassius accuses him of wrongdoing in front of the troops? Is he responding in character? How does Brutus feel about Cassius now?
2. What does Brutus mean when he says, "When love begins to sicken and decay/It useth an enforcéd ceremony."? Have you ever experienced a similar change when a friendship began to cool off? Tell about your experience.

Act IV, Scene 3

FINDING THE MAIN IDEA

1. The most important thing that happens in this scene is
   that
   (A) Brutus's and Cassius's friendship remains intact
   (B) the ghost of Caesar appears   (C) Cassius finally
   agrees with Brutus to meet Antony's army at Philippi
   (D) all of the above

REMEMBERING DETAILS

2. At the beginning of this scene, Cassius accuses Brutus of
   (A) publically condemning Lucius Pella for taking bribes
   (B) ignoring Lucius Pella   (C) putting Lucius Pella in
   prison   (D) unfair treatment of Lucius Pella
3. When Brutus says that Cassius has "an itching palm," he
   is referring to Cassius's
   (A) nervous nature   (B) selling his offices for money
   (C) allergies   (D) impatience to begin the war
4. What request had Brutus made of Cassius that he accused
   Cassius of not fulfilling?
   (A) more troops   (B) more time   (C) money to pay his
   troops   (D) none of the above
5. What does Cassius do that eases the tension between the
   two men?
   (A) he offers Brutus some wine   (B) he threatens to
   leave   (C) he takes out his dagger and asks Brutus to
   stab him in the heart   (D) he reveals his feelings of guilt

DRAWING CONCLUSIONS

6. The words, "By heaven, I had rather coin my heart/And
   drop my blood for drachmas..." reveal
   (A) how much honesty means to Cassius   (B) how much
   honesty means to Brutus   (C) how much money means
   to Brutus   (D) how much money means to Cassius

USING YOUR REASON

7. What does Cassius's request for Brutus to kill him with his dagger tell you about Cassius?
   (A) he is being hysterical   (B) he is desperate for Brutus's friendship   (C) he is daring   (D) all of the above

8. Both the actions of the triumvirs in Act I, Scene 1 and the actions of the conspirators in this scene show that power
   (A) brings out the best in people   (B) often corrupts those who hold it   (C) is the best healer of differences (D) baffles only those who do not have it

IDENTIFYING THE MOOD

9. The feelings between Brutus and Cassius in this scene shift from anger to
   (A) rage   (B) violence   (C) calm   (D) contempt

THINKING IT OVER

1. Compare how Brutus and Cassius view friendship. Which character's view of friendship is similar to your own? Do you think that sometimes you can be critical of a friend, or do good friends always overlook each other's faults? Explain your opinion.

2. Why does Shakespeare have the ghost of Caesar return at this point in the play? Who does the ghost say that he is? Is Brutus willing to meet the ghost's challenge? Why? Explain your answer.

3. What does Brutus mean when he says, "There is a tide in the affairs of men/Which, taken at the flood, leads on to fortune;/Omitted, all the voyage of their life/Is bound in shallows and in miseries."? Do you agree or disagree?

Act V, Scene 1

FINDING THE MAIN IDEA

1. The most important thing that happens in this scene is
(A) Antony and Brutus meet at Philippi   (B) Cassius
speaks about omens   (C) Brutus and Cassius speak of
death and defeat   (D) Antony says he knows what the
conspirators will do

REMEMBERING DETAILS

2. This scene takes place
(A) in Sardis   (B) in Rome   (C) on the plains of
Philippi   (D) in none of the above places
3. Brutus's and Cassius's armies
(A) stay in the hills and wait for Antony to come up for
the attack   (B) come down from the hills to meet
Antony's army   (C) make a surprise attack from behind
(D) attack from the left of the battlefield
4. Before the attack, Brutus and Antony meet and
(A) exchange insults   (B) shake hands   (C) discuss
Caesar's death   (D) compare strategies

DRAWING CONCLUSIONS

5. The fact Antony says he can read Brutus's and Cassius's
thoughts shows that
(A) he is clairvoyant   (B) he is an excellent military
strategist   (C) he is feeling extremely self-confident
(D) he has top advisors
6. The words spoken by Antony, "Why do you cross me in
this exigent?" and Octavius's response, "I do not cross
you; but I will do so" tell us that
(A) the triumvirs are of one mind   (B) the triumvirs are
not getting along   (C) the triumvirs are having a power
conflict   (D) both B and C

USING YOUR REASON

7. Which words show that Cassius feels pessimistic about the outcome of this battle?
   (A) "...ravens, crows, and kites/Fly o'er our heads and downward look on us/As we were sickly prey;" (B) "If we do lose this battle, then is this/The very last time we shall speak together" (C) "Forever, and forever, farewell, Brutus!" (D) all of the above

THINKING IT OVER

1. How do Brutus and Cassius each view defeat? Have they each decided what they will do if defeated? Are they both acting in character? Explain.
2. How do Brutus and Cassius feel toward each other in their parting words? Give at least two examples from the play to support your answer.

Act V, Scene 2

FINDING THE MAIN IDEA
1. The purpose of this brief scene is to
   (A) warn the enemy   (B) prepare the audience for the battle   (C) show Brutus's change in mood   (D) none of the above

REMEMBERING DETAILS
2. Where is Messala headed?
   (A) back to Sardis   (B) to meet the enemy   (C) to tell Cassius to begin the attack   (D) back to Rome for additional troops
3. Who spoke the words, "Ride, ride, Messala. . . ."?
   (A) Octavius   (B) Brutus   (C) Antony   (D) Cassius

DRAWING CONCLUSIONS
4. The "alarum" in this scene is
   (A) a loud shout on- or offstage signifying battle
   (B) the raising of the flags   (C) drums and trumpets sounding   (D) a clock striking

USING YOUR REASON
5. Brutus's words, ". . .for I perceive/But cold demeanor in Octavius' wing," show that
   (A) Brutus's state of mind has remained the same from the previous scene   (B) Brutus seems much more hopeful about the outcome of this battle   (C) winter weather will soon arrive   (D) Brutus would rather be in Octavius's army

THINKING IT OVER
What does Brutus mean when he says, "And sudden push gives them the overthrow."? Do you think Brutus really feels confident that they can defeat Octavius? If not, why does he appear to be so optimistic? Explain your opinion.

Act V, Scene 3

1. In this scene, the conflict between Cassius and Caesar is resolved as
   (A) Titinius dies   (B) Massala dies   (C) Cassius dies
   (D) Antony dies

2. Whom had Cassius slain just before the scene opened?
   (A) Brutus   (B) Titinius   (C) an ensign from his own
   troops (D) none of the above
3. Why does Cassius send Pindarus to a higher hill?
   (A) to see who has burned the tents   (B) to see if the
   troops are friend or enemy   (C) to watch Titinius and
   see what he finds out   (D) to signal an attack by Mark
   Antony
4. What happens to Titinius?
   (A) he is captured by the enemy   (B) he is surrounded
   by his own troops   (C) he is killed   (D) he returns with
   good news

5. When Cassius says, "My life is run his compass," he is
   talking about
   (A) living a long life   (B) his confusion about which
   direction to take   (C) the approach of his own death
   (D) the fatigue of battle
6. Cassius decides to commit suicide because
   (A) he is no longer strong enough to fight   (B) he fears
   that with Titinius's capture, defeat is not far behind
   (C) he feels he has let Brutus down   (D) he wants to die
   before being killed by the enemy
7. Titinius kills himself because
   (A) he cannot bear the pain of Cassius's death   (B) he
   feels he has let Caesar down   (C) Brutus will kill him
   anyway   (D) he has been a traitor

USING YOUR REASON

8. The words Cassius says as he is stabbed, "Caesar, thou art revenged" reveal that
   (A) he probably feels a little guilty about killing Caesar
   (B) he feels that he deserves to die because he has killed Caesar   (C) both A and B   (D) neither A nor B

9. What words show Brutus's feelings about who still holds the power in all that has happened in Rome?
   (A) "Alas, thou hast misconstrued everything!"   (B) "O hateful Error, Melancholy's child,"   (C) "O Julius Caesar, thou art mighty yet!"   (D) "I shall find time, Cassius; I shall find time."

THINKING IT OVER

1. How does Brutus feel about Cassius's death? What does he say about Cassius as a fellow Roman? Do you agree with Brutus? Explain your opinion.

2. What is really being decided at the battle of Philippi? Does Shakespeare give any clues as to which side he favors? Explain your answer.

3. How might the events in the plot have been different if Pindarus or Cassius had not misinterpreted what happened to Titinius? Describe an alternative outcome for this scene.

Act V, Scene 4

FINDING THE MAIN IDEA

1. This scene is mostly concerned with preparing the audience for
   (A) the end of the battle   (B) the resolution of the final conflict   (C) Brutus's death   (D) all of the above

REMEMBERING DETAILS

2. Lucilius compares Cato's death with
   (A) his own   (B) Cassius's   (C) Titinius's   (D) Cato's father's

3. Lucilius tricks the enemy soldiers into thinking he is
   (A) Titinius   (B) Cato   (C) Brutus   (D) none of the above

4. Antony wants Lucilius
   (A) to be killed   (B) to be treated kindly   (C) to be taken prisoner   (D) to rejoin Brutus's army

DRAWING CONCLUSIONS

5. Lucilius tricked the soldiers in order to
   (A) allow time for Antony to approach   (B) help Cato
   (C) allow time for Brutus to escape   (D) none of the above

THINKING IT OVER

What two choices are now left for Brutus? Which choice do you think he will make? Why?

Act V, Scene 5

FINDING THE MAIN IDEA

1. In this scene, the final conflict of the play is resolved between
   (A) Antony and Octavius (B) Cassius and Brutus
   (C) Caesar and Brutus (D) Caesar and Antony

REMEMBERING DETAILS

2. Whom does Brutus ask to kill him?
   (A) Clitis (B) Dardanius (C) Volumnius (D) all of the above
3. How does Brutus finally die?
   (A) Antony's soldiers wound him (B) Strato holds Brutus's sword and he runs upon it (C) Marsalla stabs him in the back (D) none of the above
4. To whom does Brutus speak as he dies?
   (A) Strato (B) Caesar (C) Cassius (D) Octavius

DRAWING CONCLUSIONS

5. You can figure out that the reason three people refused to kill Brutus is that
   (A) they are extremely loyal to him (B) they do not want to be accused of murder (C) they fear Antony's revenge (D) they are too frightened

USING YOUR REASON

6. In his final words about Brutus, "This was the noblest Roman of them all," Antony reveals that he
   (A) held Brutus in high regard (B) felt Brutus acted honorably (C) felt Brutus acted unselfishly (D) all of the above
7. Caesar's ghost, or Caesar's spirit, that appears in the play actually may be
   (A) a dream (B) a vision (C) Brutus's conscience
   (D) an omen

THINKING IT OVER

1. Who do you think is the hero of the play and who is the villain? Why? Explain your opinion.
2. Why do you think Octavius speaks the final words in the play? Is there a double meaning to his use of the word *part*? Who do you think will finally lead Rome? Why?